MASTER — YOUR — MIND

MASTER YOUR MIND

Counterintuitive Strategies to Refocus and Re-Energize Your Runaway Brain

ROGER SEIP
ROBB ZBIERSKI

WILEY

Published by John Wiley & Sons, Inc., Hoboken, New Jersey.
Published simultaneously in Canada.

For general information on our other products and services or for technical support, please contact our Customer Care Department within the United States at (800) 762-2974, outside the United States at (317) 572-3993 or fax (317) 572-4002.

Wiley also publishes its books in a variety of electronic formats. Some content that appears in print may not be available in electronic formats. For more information about Wiley products, visit our web site at www.wiley.com.

Library of Congress Cataloging-in-Publication Data is Available:

ISBN 9781394190218 (Paperback)
ISBN 9781119508175 (ePub)
ISBN 9781119508168 (ePDF)

Cover design: Wiley

SKY10054606_090423

This book is dedicated to everyone who kept asking me, "When is your book coming out?"

—Robb Zbierski

Contents

Introduction

Need speed? Slow down.

—David Allen, Getting Things Done

Roger's Story of "Slowing Down to Speed Up"

Life and business lessons come to us at the weirdest times. The idea for this book hit me when I was passed by a 78-year-old grandma on the running trail.

I'd been trying unsuccessfully to train for a marathon for a couple of years. I'd actually run a couple and was trying to get back into shape to run a personal best, and I hadn't been making any real progress. The trouble was that I kept getting injured – first a foot, then a knee, then a hip – and each injury would sideline me from running for a couple months. And then I'd have to start training all over again. It was this constant process of one step forward, two steps back.

In trying to figure out how to be a faster runner with more endurance, I read a number of books that espoused the idea of training at an incredibly slow pace to ultimately get faster. When I first stumbled onto this teaching, it made no sense at all. I'd always been taught that if you want to *go* faster, you *train* faster. Going *slow* to go *fast* sounds totally counterintuitive and backward, right?

Well, the thing is, it actually works. Since this isn't really a running book, I won't get into all the nerdball science of why it works, but here's the short version:

For running anything longer than about a mile, you must rely on your body's aerobic system. That's the energy production system in your body that allows you to burn fat for fuel and use oxygen most efficiently, and is best developed by making yourself train at a pace that does raises your heart rate, but only to a level where you're not even breathing very hard. For me, that was a pace that was painfully, agonizingly, embarrassingly s-l-o-o-o-w. The idea is that running while keeping your heart rate in this Target Zone allows your aerobic system to develop. As your aerobic system gets stronger and more turned on, your body starts using oxygen more efficiently and your speed naturally increases. Like I said, it seemed a little backwards, but here I was not really getting anywhere with what I was doing, so I thought, "Okay, what have I got to lose?"

For me that process ultimately transformed (and is actually still transforming) me into a faster runner, but it's a very incremental process, especially at first. It's also a humbling process – it ain't sexy. After just a few weeks of consistent but v-e-r-r-r-ry slow running, my commitment was put to the test by a cute little old lady.

Keep in mind, I've been an athlete since I was 15 years old. Not a great athlete by any stretch, but an athlete nonetheless. I'm intentional about my physical fitness and I'm competitive. So as I'm leisurely jogging along one morning (training slow, keeping the heart rate down, right?), you can imagine that I'm getting passed by people on the trail. When the 20-something 6-foot-4 dude with the beautiful gazelle-like stride and the "University of Wisconsin Track Team" T-shirt whipped by, I was not embarrassed. Shortly thereafter, when the 30-something grad student passed me up, I remained unconcerned. But when the 4-and-a-half-foot-tall granny caught me from behind, I started having a little problem with my ego. Don't get me wrong, she was super nice and gave me a lovely smile as she ran by – but she promptly left me in the dust.

I couldn't believe it. I had just been smoked by a runner twice my age!

(Side note: Can we please set aside the idea that my outrage was totally ridiculous? I'm aware of how silly I was being. I mean, we weren't actually even in a race, but still, a guy's gotta have standards.)

The best thing that this small incident brought about was that it made me look at what I was doing. Unnecessary as it was, I got worked up enough to ask "Is this training slow thing even *working*?!" And, miracle of miracles, I learned that it really was. My mile time at my target heart rate had improved by well over a minute per mile, after just a few weeks. I had felt embarrassed for a moment, but the actual results told me the truth.

Slowing down my running had made me a faster runner. Unbelievable.

Then lightbulbs started going off in my brain, and I began to see all the connections to how the principle – slow down in order to get faster – was actually a full-fledged Law of Life. It became very clear that this was in fact a bedrock practice that had consistently paid massive dividends in my business, with my family, in my income, and literally in every area of my life.

In that moment I even had some flashbacks. I remembered when my great mentor, Dan Moore, in my first sales career, taught me the "Rocket/Snail" philosophy, in which you move like a rocket in between conversations with prospects but slow down to a snail's pace when you're actually in those conversations. I remembered another mentor, Janet Attwood, who taught me "Intention, Attention, No Tension," which involves a combination of working intently while simultaneously relaxing your way to success. The whole concept of a Flow State – the optimal performance mindset that many call being "In the Zone" – became much clearer to me. I noticed how every major breakthrough I'd ever experienced – periods where money and business results were materializing so fast I could barely keep up – had been brought about by *slowing down.* It was totally counterintuitive . . . it didn't make logical sense and it seemed backward, but the evidence was irrefutable.

Slowing down my Runaway Brain (and thereby slowing down the game) had made me a faster results-getter, in every single area of my life. When I slowed down and used the methods and understandings in this book, business and life just worked so much better:

much more productive, much more elegant and effortless, much less frustrated/stressed. And isn't that what we're all looking for?

Roger's Note

The whole concept of "slowing down to speed up" will be a strong recurring theme of this book. In fact, the original title of *Master Your Mind* was going to be *The Snail and the Rocket,* because it was going to be all about this premise. In the writing and editing of the book, the title, and the cover, we found that overt references to "slowing down to speed up" morphed into other things, but please don't miss this critical lesson. Both neuroscience and the experiences of our coaching clients teach us that getting the results you want, as fast as you want, almost always requires that you slow things down.

Robb's Story

"HEY-Y-Y!"

The sound of 200 high schoolers screaming in unison echoed through the gym. My mind raced as I knew what was coming next and I was not excited about it. I sat back just a smidge, enough to see the backs of the ears of the kids on either side of me. Enough to where they couldn't see that I wasn't going to participate. It was our side's turn.

This is stupid, I thought. Why are we screaming at each other using nonsense words? How is this going to help me? Why did the school bring this guy in to make us look like idiots in front of each other? My rambling thoughts were interrupted by a loud "BOOM-BAH!!"

Classmates all around me screamed at the top of their lungs, as if trying to knock the other kids out of the bleachers.

"HEY-Y-Y!" came the other side's response.

Everyone laughed, I even laughed, and then it hit me.

I'm missing out.

So I waited. And slowed down. And listened. The speaker started making sense. If you spent less time worrying about looking like an idiot and more time actually enjoying the moment, life is going to get a *lot* easier. After all, we were 400 kids all looking like idiots together and having a blast doing it. Well, at least 399 were enjoying it. I missed out.

And that was my first lesson on slowing down in order to accelerate my results. This idea is presented in a lot of ways in a lot of situations and with a lot of people. But when you slow down your thoughts, slow down your perceptions, slow down your beliefs, slow down the stories in your head, and in a lot of cases slow down your actions, that is the first step in stepping out of your own way and living the life you want to lead.

Over the years, the idea got buried under the load of a ton of random jobs and experiences. Grocery-store stockboy, landscaper, bike shop employee, facility services coordinator (read: help run the custodial staff at a Big-10 school), computer lab manger, PR intern, event coordinator, advocacy coordinator, project manager, sales manager, global marketing manager, and probably a bunch more I've forgotten, either on purpose or accidentally.

In every single one of these jobs, I often found myself jammed somewhere between "We're going *way* too fast" and "Hurry up, we need to get this done!" In either one of those extremes, it's a tiny reminder that the most rapid pace isn't what's needed. And I'm reminded of this almost daily in the conversations I have with folks from all different types of backgrounds, professions and educational levels. It's a common theme in life. Folks are either going too fast or they can't keep up and it always feels like they are out of control. It's not sustainable, and it's time to take control.

I've been asked to write a book for years. Friends, family, and clients have all asked, "So, when is your book coming out?" For years I never had an answer. I never felt like I had anything original or interesting to share. Or I was too busy to write one. After all, no one wants to read the same rehashed stuff they have heard before. And then a funny thing occurred to me.

I'm missing out. And maybe someone else is, as well.

So here it is. My hope is that this book helps you become more *acceptional* in your life. I coined this term by combining *accepting* and *exceptional.* I do believe that when you simply slow down, take a step back, think about and accept more in your life, then your life can become exceptional.

So slow down and enjoy the read. Hopefully you will find a few nuggets for yourself. Because you never know when you might have the opportunity to scream at the top of your lungs with those around you. Imagine doing that with zero inhibitions and creating a memory that lasts forever! Or you might hold back. And I promise you'll get a memory out of that experience, as well.

Getting Results Faster . . . What Does That Mean?

If you're reading this book, it's a certainty that achieving results is really important to you . . . indeed, you're probably kind of obsessed. See, we've built a company and a ton of content specifically for businesspeople and professionals who absolutely must get results. Likely you fall into one of these categories:

- You're a sales professional of some kind – financial advisor, realtor, insurance agent, pharmaceutical rep, or some other position where your role is building a book of business. You may or may not get paid on commission, but there's a strong element of your professional life that involves the concept of "you eat what you kill." There's a very direct connection between how well you perform at work and how well you and your family live.
- You own a business or you're a credentialled professional of some kind. We work with a lot of traditional and nontraditional business owners, a lot of executives, a lot of doctors, attorneys, dentists, accountants, and the like. You may not consider yourself a salesperson, in fact you may shy away from anything that smells like selling, but nonetheless … your career requires that you get results with and for your customers, clients or patients.

Either way, the deal is that you need to make things – tangible things – happen daily, right? You've got:

- Quotas to hit
- Goals to achieve
- Teams to build
- Clients/patients to serve
- Money to make
- Projects to finish
- Deadlines to hit
- Races to win

And on and on ... and you probably don't want to burn out while doing it. You're looking to get positive results in a way that feels fantastic, right? You're not afraid of working hard to accomplish your goals, but you're also not super interested in killing yourself in the process. You're looking for some version of harmony in your life, not simply working, working, working on the hamster wheel. Absolutely you want to be wealthy, you want to "make it," but you know there's much more to life than just money. As you look forward a year or two (or more), you want to see a life of real prosperity, real enthusiasm, real peace of mind . . . real *winning* in all aspects of your life.

Less Really Can Be More

So if that's what you're looking for, let's be clear that the answer is not just *more activity*. You kind of sensed that, right? Don't get us wrong, you will need to put forth a significant, in fact sometimes *massive* effort to achieve significant things. If you came here looking for magic formulas that require no effort, you've come to the wrong place. Work is necessary, work is foundational, work is good.

What we're saying is that the solution to the problem of getting where you really want to go *isn't solely about quantity of effort* . . . it can't be. The math only works up to a certain point. Example:

If you're currently working 50 hours a week (many of you are) and you want to double your income, one way to accomplish that would be to double the number of hours you work. Mathematically that could work, but there are two glaring problems with this strategy.

1. Working 100 hours a week is brutally exhausting. And considering there are only 168 hours in a week, you can't really do anything except work and sleep.

2. What happens when you want to double your income again? It's impossible to work 200 hours a week, s-o-o-o . . . whatcha gonna do now?

Of course this is a grossly oversimplified example, but you get the idea.

Look at your endeavors as having a "threshold of effort." If you're below that threshold, improvement is in fact about elevating the *quantity* of your effort. If you're a financial advisor in the first few years of your practice, you will need to work a lot of hours and generate a lot of activity or you will fail. If you're an athlete, you will require a huge volume of practice and training effort. In any quest for results, you have to reach that Effort Threshold first. So if you're currently below that threshold, focus on getting over that line. *Master Your Mind* can still help you – just make sure you're meeting that threshold as a foundation.

Because once you get over that threshold, improvement ceases to be about quantity – it then immediately becomes all about improving the *quality* of your effort. It becomes about your focus, your skill, your presence, your intentionality, and your mastery of dropping into that mythical state known as The Zone.

And when you start upgrading these things – the focus, the skill, the presence, and so on – results can expand both exponentially and infinitely. You remove the ceiling, because there is no ceiling on mastery. When our hard-working clients start focusing this way, their quantifiable results improve so quickly that it's often quite startling. They see business revenue shoot through the roof. They see incomes double, triple, and even quadruple within a year. Customer service ratings skyrocket, recruiting becomes exponentially more effective, and bottom line results simply *spike*. And the key is that we see this all take place *with little or no extra effort.*

More important, the upgrades you'll learn here will make you feel amazing! Our clients often experience the unusual sensation of having more energy at the *end* of the day than they did at the *beginning* (wait … what?). They're keenly aware that what they're doing is fully streamlined, because it is:

- Aligned with what's most deeply important to them
- Being done in a way that actually works for their brain

So it legitimately feels like some kind of magic, but it's not. Learning how to combine the right amount of effort with a high degree of presence, focus, intentionality, and "Zone-itude" means that you end up making it look easy … which makes sense when you understand how your Runaway Brain likes to be harnessed.

And the key to all of these performance optimizers – presence, focus, intentionality, being in The Zone – you know the common theme to getting more of them?

They all require slowing down.

They require slowing down "the game" and literally slowing down your own Runaway Brain. If you want to get results exponentially faster, *you're gonna need to slow down.*

Slow down to speed up . . . that sounds counterintuitive, but it works.

How to Get the Most from This Book

If you've read our first bestselling book *Train Your Brain for Success*, you noticed that it was a lot like a workbook in many places. (By the way, if you've *not* read *Train Your Brain for Success*, it would be a great idea to buy it and read it soon – just sayin'.) This book is a little different, and should actually be even easier to digest. Here's how to get the most from this learning experience.

Tip #1: Just Read the Book

Really – just read it at your own pace. Some folks take great books and devour them all in one sitting ... If that's you, fantastic. Others will take a few chapters at a time and savor this book over a few weeks or a few months. This is also a fine way to digest this material. There's really no "wrong" way to read this, unless you just let it sit on your shelf. If you want to maximize the value of your reading, it would be a good idea to have a highlighter and a pen handy to jot down some notes (actually those are great ways to slow down), but fundamentally, simply make sure you're actually reading this book.

Tip for Even More Speed

Master Your Mind is broken up into two parts after this introduction:

> Part I: Slow Down Your Brain, which gives you a much better understanding of what's really going on in your head that gets results . . . and what hold you back.
>
> Part II: Slow Down the Game, which is the specific methods and tactics we teach our clients in workshops and coaching relationships.

Part I, to provide the foundation for tactics (the "Why this stuff works") has some science in it- we're not scientists per se, but most of our clients find it helpful to know at least some basic brain science. Simultaneously, we're all about application and putting these methods to work. You don't need to understand the workings of an internal combustion engine in order to drive your car. So, we'd highly recommend reading Part I- gaining the understanding of your root causes is pretty important. But if you're just bored to tears with science, or if you're just like "Dudes, I need action steps NOW!!!" . . . . feel free to go directly to Part II, get things working and then develop the science-y understanding later.

Tip #2: As You're Reading, Be Actively Looking for a Small Number of Things to Implement Right Away

There's a lot that'll get served up in these pages. You'll gain new understandings of how the deep part of your brain works, you'll receive some real wisdom from some of our clients' examples, and you'll learn some hyper-effective techniques that have proven to produce far better results both immediately and in the long term.

In our live workshops and keynotes, we often see our clients fall into the trap of getting all fired up and then trying to do too much. The thought process would sound like this:

> Oh man, this is awesome. I'm gonna do *everything* different! Wake up different, go to bed different, talk different, think different, act different, all day long … I'm just gonna do *everything* different!"

No, you're not. Really, you're just not going to do everything different, and that's okay. You probably don't *need* to do everything different, and you definitely don't need to do a half-assed job of doing "everything" different. Most likely you need to get really serious about doing a small number of things differently.

What's a small number? One or two. If this book helps you upgrade one or two practices or thought patterns, that's likely all you need in order to start seeing massively upgraded results. So, we'll say it again: *One* or *two* things to either think about or do differently is what you're looking for here. Deal?

Tip #3: Get Going, and Embrace the Ugly

When you identify something to work on here, you'll get maximum benefit if you take some action on it immediately. As a result of reading this book, it's likely that you'll want to change something. As an example, we often see our coaching clients upgrade:

- How you wake up
- How you go to sleep

- How you structure your weekly plan
- How you talk to yourself or about yourself
- How you connect your activities with your purpose
- How you do a "to-do" list or a "to-not-do" list
- What you say "yes" to and "no" to

Or it could be any number of things, too numerous to list here. There are dozens (if not hundreds) of possibilities laid out in these pages that you could use to make a shift. The point is, when one of these possibilities resonates with you, *do* something about it as soon as possible. If you want to change how you wake up, do it the very next time you wake up. If you decide you want to operate with a Two-Hour Solution plan for your week, make that plan right away. It's a great idea to start with a small step, but most important, *take the step*.

Two additional things about taking action:

1. Whatever action step you choose, do it consistently for at least 30 days; 60 to 90 days would be even better. One of the things that our coaching allows clients to do is to physically rewire their brains, and thereby recalibrate their internal "set point" to a higher level of performance that sticks. The key to accomplishing this kind of rewiring is that it can not happen all at once. Rewiring your brain (a.k.a. establishing a new habit) requires at minimum around 30 days of consistent action, and 90 days is a safer bet.

2. When you start acting on the principles you learn here, be prepared for to feel fairly uncomfortable at first. The methods we use are deceptively simple, and definitely counterintuitive. Truthfully, some of them just aren't that sexy, and so they might feel awkward at first. You might even get some resistance, either from that "little voice in your head" (more on that later) or even from the people in your world. You may or may not have people tell you that you're a little nuts, but if you do, please understand that this is normal and is actually a sign of your growth.

So let's dive in!

PART I

Slow Down Your Brain: Let an Elephant Do Your Work for You

In Part I of *Master Your Mind*, we'll lay the foundation for *why* you and your brain need to slow down. This foundation will be both scientific and anecdotal in nature – we'll draw from the latest research in neuroscience and quantum physics, plus the practical experiences of our clients and ourselves.

Our aim with Part I is to help you understand *you* a little better.

You're going to learn about how your brain operates on its deepest levels (hint: It's not just a little different, it's often the exact opposite of what we see on the surface). You'll learn about what happens when your brain physically slows down the frequency at which it vibrates. You'll also identify some of the "default settings" we're all preprogrammed with, and gain some understanding into how to stop sabotaging yourself.

We believe you'll find Part I to be not just interesting on an academic level, but enlightening on a personal level, and extremely practical in your day-to-day activities. Enjoy!

1

Slowing Down, Speeding Up, and Your "Runaway Brain" . . . What Are We Talking About?

There is no such thing as overtraining . . . just underresting.

—*Allen Lim, PhD founder, Skratch Labs*

Slowing Down . . . What's That Mean?

From Robb:

Having spent almost a decade in the cycling industry, I had so many opportunities to learn about slowing down in order to speed up. But my thoughts were usually going so fast I probably missed most of them. That is, until my friend Allen Lim dropped this nugget on me one day. Dr. Lim is one of the world's leading authorities on exercise physiology, specifically in bicycling. Anyone outside of cycling may not know his name, but if we were to rattle off a list of athletes who have hired him to help them win races, medals, competitions, or contracts, that would be a heck of a list.

I first heard him say this right after he had finished consulting for a Tour de France team years ago. He was sharing his months-long experience with us and throughout the course of his stories, his quote made more and more sense.

For those who are unaware, and regardless of your opinion of cycling, the Tour de France is arguably one of the hardest, most grueling events in all of sports. And it requires quite an investment of suffering in order to complete the event. Competitors typically ride a minimum of 100 miles every day for three weeks straight. There are only two days off. The stages typically include climbing, sprinting, hours-long turns riding at the front to block the wind, and countless trips back and forth to the team car to gather food, water, and supplies. Got a bee sting? Road rash? Sunburn? Saddle sore? (Yes, that's a real thing and at least as painful as you can imagine it to be.) Too bad. You must deal with it and fight through the pain, because many of the medicines used to heal these problems are banned in and out of competition.

So Al was sharing with us that his job is to help the riders figure out ways to stay healthy and strong up to and through the last week of the race. A lot of riders believe that they need to grind it out no matter what, all day and every day. They have been told "it will only make me stronger for tomorrow, so harden the "f" up!" This is a mindset that many professionals carry into their sales, customer service, clinical, insurance, real estate, and trade careers. Spoiler alert: There's always a story about failure or burnout that follows the admission.

Al's job was to help the athletes learn, understand, and apply different techniques for doing just the right amount of work exactly when they needed to while racing, so that their bodies could fully recover between stages. Climbers should ride their hardest only in the climbs. Sprinters can sit in until the last possible moment. Domestiques (the guys who do all the grunt work and protect the team leader[s]) can take turns, never going a minute longer than they need to at the front of the pack.

The lesson for these cyclists is this: You think you are tired from working too hard. That's only part of it. You are actually tired from not taking the proper amount of time to recover. You waste energy doing things you don't need to do to achieve the goal. And then you don't value your "down time" enough to let yourself rest and recover properly. You are already thinking about tomorrow when you haven't even finished today. You're not fully present where you are *right now*, and instead you are creating turbulence, and *that's* what's exhausting you.

Cure for the Common "GO!"

Here's the deal: most of you reading this book aren't cyclists. But the lesson is still relevant for you, personally and professionally. Replace the word "cyclist" with "realtor" or "financial advisor" or "artist" or whatever your profession or your goal is.

Imagine a financial advisor studying for her Series 65. She spends a *ton* of time studying, typically after a full workday. She tries reading when she is tired. Her mind is elsewhere. She forgets what she read. And this happens over and over and over again. She starts thinking about what will happen if she doesn't get her studying done. It stresses her out. She stays up late and doesn't get a good night sleep. Every single appointment the next day is unproductive. Are you starting to see how the idea of "powering through" isn't serving you? Are you starting to notice that taking a little more "down time" will help you operate more effectively during your "up time"?

Stop trying to "fight through" to get what you want. Stop ignoring reality. Start rethinking how you approach things. Start putting the appropriate amount of time, effort, and mental bandwidth into not only working smarter but also thinking smarter. *Thinking smarter* means less small thinking and more *big* thinking, less overthinking, and more relaxing.

Real-Life Examples

When it comes to slowing down in order gain progress, there are examples we can find everywhere to understand the importance of this tactic.

An airline pilot's job is to safely travel from origin to the destination. If he can make it there on time, that's a bonus! But the ultimate goal is to get the plane safely to the destination.

How many times have you been on the plane, in your seat, slightly overheated, wondering when this plane is going to take off. All of a sudden the sweet, soothing sound of "Boi-n-n-ng" comes over the loudspeaker, followed by "Ladies and gentleman, this is your Captain speaking. We are currently number 12 for takeoff, but don't worry, we'll make it up in the air. So for now, just go ahead and sit back and relax, we'll be off the ground in just a bit."

You might think the pilot needs to speed up in order to achieve his goal. He needs to fly faster than he had planned in order to get to the destination on time. But there's more at stake here.

The pilot needs to get to the airspace where the destination air-traffic controller can get the plane in the queue to land. Once there, the pilot receives instructions on where to be and when (and at what speed) in order to keep the air traffic flowing smoothly.

Here's the best and potentially most overlooked part. In order for the pilot to achieve the goal (landing safely at the destination), the most important thing he needs to do is slow the plane down. If the pilot does not decrease the speed of the plane, it literally can't land, and he'll never achieve the goal.

How many projects, conversations, activities, meetings, and so on never got finished simply because you never took a second to "lay off the gas" in order to let things fall into place, instead of having the emergency brake pulled, bringing everything to a screeching halt?

Here's another example from football (the American type, not soccer). In order to snap the ball and start the play, everyone on the offense needs to be standing still. If someone on the offense rushes to start the play, they are penalized and subsequently get moved further from their goal. Even taking two to three seconds to stop and think can mean the difference between one step forward instead of two steps back.

Ever driven in the snow? If you have, you know that the worst thing you can do when sliding on a slippery surface is to steer the car back in the lane as hard as you can. If you haven't driven in the snow, I'll describe what happens. Your car is on its own course. All 100–200 pounds of you is *not* going to be able to get the two to three tons of automobile back on the road. No matter how hard you try or how fast you steer, you simply have to slow the car down. Only then can the tires grab and allow you to regain control. The car is downright out of control until you slow it down and take control of it.

Your mind operates the same way, and if allowed to careen along it can become a Runaway Brain. This is what we'll be talking about in the next few pages.

What's a "Runaway Brain" and Why Should You Care?

Take this yes/no quiz:

- Have you ever met someone for the first time, shook their hand, repeated their name, and then literally five seconds later you couldn't remember their name?
- Have you ever been reading something, reached the end of a page, and realized that your mind had been . . . elsewhere, and as a result you had zero idea what you'd just "read"?
- Have you ever had a day at work when you worked to the point of exhaustion, and then realized that you had just run in circles all day and therefore didn't actually accomplish anything?
- Have you ever woken up in the middle of the night and then not been able to get back to sleep because your mind was racing about something work related?

It's likely you answered yes to all four of these, but even if you said yes to only one question, you've experienced Runaway Brain.

How Your Brain "Runs Away"

Your brain "runs away" in two ways: Sometimes it runs away like a dog runs away – you open the door, the dog squeezes out between your legs, and it just bolts. And then it keeps on going over the horizon, leaving you wondering whether you'll ever see it again. It just . . . leaves.

When your brain runs away in this sense, it shows up as

- Forgetfulness
- Being at a loss for words
- Not knowing an answer to a test question
- Wondering "Where did the day go?"
- Feeling like you're losing it, or like something might be seriously wrong

More often, your brain "runs away" with you in tow, and this is a serious problem. Lots of psychologists and authors have described how your mind can "hijack" you: It doesn't leave you – it's much more like a carjacking while you're still in the car. In this case, your thoughts are literally in the driver's seat. You may not like where you're going or the route you're taking to get there, but you're just along for the ride with no control.

If your brain is running away in this manner, you'll experience:

- Insomnia caused by a racing mind
- A lot of stress
- You'll be frustrated, irritable, and angry
- Exhaustion and burnout
- A sense of powerlessness
- Anxiety
- Distraction
- Poor self-discipline and bad time management
- Other issues that make you feel like you're driving yourself crazy and can't stop

Either way, it's not pleasant. What you may already understand is that *the Runaway Brain is not only unpleasant, it's extremely expensive*. If you are who we believe you are, things like anxiety, distraction, low energy, and forgetfulness will *cost you.* Your Runaway Brain will cost you in terms of

- Wasted time
- Destruction of personal and professional relationships
- Shrinking sales numbers
- Higher attrition or turnover
- Lowered income
- Fading self-confidence

And, clearly, nobody wants that, right?

The bad news is that we're actually *wired* to have Runaway Brains. You'll learn about your brain's unhelpful default settings in Chapter 4, for now just understand we all have strong tendencies ingrained in us which cause us to just . . . keep . . . making . . . these mistakes over and over again, until we fix the underlying cause. The good news is that you definitely *can* fix the underlying cause, which is what the rest of *Master Your Mind* is about!

A Brief Word of Caution

Actually, for refocusing and re-energizing your Runaway Brain, it's important to know how to deal with the resistance you may experience. There will be people along the way who think you're nuts, so let's take some time here and understand why all this is "counterintuitive" in the first place . . .

Know That You Can Rewire Your Brain

For most people (a.k.a. "The Majority"), a *ton* of what they think they know about life is just flat-out wrong.

You'll get way more out of this book – in fact, you'll get way more out of your life – if you are open to the idea that a *huge* percentage of the things we've been taught, been sold, or had drilled into our heads as "facts" . . . are simply not true. They often are easy to believe because they sound logical, but these inaccuracies can have negative and even devastating effects on our lives.

(*continued*)

(continued)

Some examples from different areas:

- Most of us were taught by our parents that we shouldn't go swimming for 30 minutes after we eat, because we will suffer from stomach cramps and drown. This is easy to believe because eating food makes you heavier, and heavy things sink more easily that lighter things, right? True, but this is just BS. Swimming after you eat has proven to be no problem at all, and believing this "fact" just kept us rule-followers from having fun swimming for a lot of half-hours. We are sure that our moms had good intentions, but this is an exaggeration that was passed down for generations and taught to us as truth. And really, this one's fairly inconsequential . . . the next one, however, has gigantic implications.
- For decades, the entire medical and health system (some call it the medical-industrial complex) has promoted the idea that a high carbohydrate/low-fat diet is the best way to fuel your body, be healthy, avoid heart disease, and even lose weight. We were taught to avoid fat like the plague, because "fat clogs your arteries" and "eating fat makes you fat." Again, easy to believe, right? It just sounds like it should make sense: "Eating fat makes you fat" sounds so logical that it *must* be true. Unfortunately, it's patently false for the majority of human beings. More and more research (and our own personal experience) proves that the best diet for weight loss, being healthy and alleviating everything from heart disease to diabetes to any number of chronic health issues, is a diet that includes almost no carbohydrates but relies on large amounts of high-quality fat. The reality is that eating fat actually makes you thin and healthy . . . but eating *sugar* makes you fat and chronically ill. This incorrect premise, which has been systematically sold to the public, has had gigantic implications for millions of people. Ever since the American "food pyramid" was popularized, rates of heart disease, obesity, diabetes, cancer and all manner of chronic illness have skyrocketed and become a global pandemic. Thankfully, this one is actually the subject of numerous books and a growing body of research, so I'll leave it alone for now, but the next one directly relates to your brain and your success.
- If you're like us, you were taught in school that once you reach adulthood, your brain becomes "set." We were taught that you stop making new brain cells, that your brain's structures

become fixed, and you've got what you've got. The logical extension is that learning new things becomes impossible and that your path in life is pretty much established by your early to mid 20s. Once again, this makes sense . . . and is total BS. It might be true that teaching old dogs new tricks is difficult, but you are not a dog. You're a human being, and one fantastic thing about human beings is called *neuroplasticity.* Read on . . .

Neuroplasticity was discovered in the 1980s, and it's revolutionized how we think about success, personal development, and aging. Neuroplasticity is the truth that the human brain can and does both generate new brain cells and rewire itself *throughout a person's entire lifespan.* Neural pathways can be established, re-established, and modified at will, no matter how old or young we are, no matter our race or gender, and no matter our educational background.

Do some brains require more work to "rewire" than others? Of course. But if you're able to read this book (clearly we're talking to *you*), you unquestionably have the ability to rewire your brain, and therefore you will see results, no matter where you're starting from. So please don't let other people's uninformed (or worse, *mis*informed) opinions of "what works and what doesn't" deter you in your quest for greatness. And definitely don't let "The Majority" dictate your actions . . . "they" may not be in doubt, but they're often wrong.

Why did we create such a lengthy sidebar? Because you have to understand that when you take action on new things that will transform and elevate you, you will encounter resistance. Because everyone has been exposed to myths and exaggerations and believed them, and when you start to break away from the established norms, you become a rebel. You become "not normal." Those who are *not* deviating from the norm (a.k.a. "The Majority") often subconsciously feel threatened by your new path. If this happens, they may sometimes attack you. How will you know if this is happening?

As you start refocusing and re-energizing your Runaway Brain, you will notice that:

- You have more energy.
- You sleep better at night.

- You're much more productive – you accomplish more in less time.
- You're happier.
- You have much greater control over your life, more enthusiasm, and more peace of mind.
- You're literally more magnetic and attractive to high-caliber people.

On the flip side, you may simultaneously notice that:

- You hear people make some jokes about "Mr./Ms. Positive."
- Some people in your circle of friends start seeming tiresome and draining to you.
- Those around you get sucked into drama that you used to be interested in, but no longer are.
- Some long-standing relationships change or maybe even disappear.

If/when you experience these flip sides, do not let them stop you – please just notice that they're happening, realize that they're happening *because you're growing*, and *stay the course.* You may need to enlist the help of a coach or mentor to keep on track, but please stay the course. These reactions in your environment will be temporary storms that subside, and when they do you'll be in such a much better place.

So let's get cracking, shall we? We'll begin this journey by helping you to understand more deeply what's actually going on in your brain, specifically the parts of your brain that actually get results. Some of it might seem backward, odd, or counterintuitive, but you're about to learn quite a bit about *you*. Here we go!

Chapter Review

- There's no such thing as going too hard, but there's definitely such a thing as not going slow enough.
- Land the plane.
- Get set before the ball is hiked.
- It's going to be difficult at first. Observe the friction instead of fighting it.

2

Understanding and Harnessing Your Subconscious Brain

The Mind is like an iceberg – it floats with only one seventh of its bulk above the water."

—*Sigmund Freud, founder of psychoanalysis*

One of our favorite things that we see happening for our clients is that they do things like double their business while also taking three-day (or even four-day) weekends nearly every week. This cannot be done by simply "working harder" or being "more intense". No, in order to achieve these ninja-like levels of efficiency and speed, the best way to is to make a quantum leap. You literally have to find a whole new gear in your engine – one that we all have, but most of us are not aware of.

This gear is called your subconscious brain.

Likely you've heard this term before, but it's also likely you're not fully aware of how your subconscious works, or how gigantically powerful it is when it comes to making results happen. Think about the word itself: "subconscious" literally means "below consciousness," so everything that it does, it does without you even being aware of it. When you're letting your subconscious do its job, the hallmark is that good things happen and it feels like you did nothing. Sales get made, deals get done, and awards get won, but the experience is one of complete effortlessness. Here's why this is, along with how to harness the power of an elephant.

You see, the conscious part of your brain and the subconscious (or unconscious or nonconscious or whichever term you prefer) are intertwined, but they are not the same. They have completely different functions, completely different purposes, and they do different jobs. They're even located in different parts of your physical brain. In many cases the methods to harness these two components of your brain are in fact polar opposites – what works well for your conscious can often be totally counterproductive for your subconscious.

We could spend the rest of this book and several others on discussing the brain science behind these differences. This book is about the practical applications, so let's understand the basic differences in plain English; check out Table 2.1.

Table 2.1 Differences between the Conscious and Subconscious

	Conscious	**Subconscious**
Runs on . . .	Logic	Emotion
Good at . . .	Judging/evaluating	Moving/acts
Right vs. wrong . . .	Moral	Amoral
Useful for . . .	Setting goals	Achieving goals
Engage it for . . .	Training	Performing
Thinks in . . .	Words/sentences	Pictures
Perception of time . . .	Sees past, present, future	Always now
Governs your . . .	Reason	Intuition

Four Key Differences between the Conscious and Subconscious Brains

Guess what . . . you actually have *two* brains! There's the "conscious" part, which is the part you're aware of. It's also the part that we tend to identify with most often. When we "think of thinking," what we're usually talking about is our conscious brain.

But then there's your *sub*conscious, the part that's literally below your conscious awareness. Very much like when you study subatomic particles (which act *very* differently from atoms, molecules, and larger structures), your subconscious brain acts *very* differently from the part you're aware of. Let's explore how that works, and what that means for your results. The following sections are about the four key differences between your conscious and subconscious brains.

Difference #1: Your Subconscious Is Orders of Magnitude Larger Than Your Conscious

Amazing fact about your brain: You've got roughly 100 billion brain cells running around upstairs. That's a staggering number to begin with, and it gets downright mind-boggling when you realize that they're all connected to each other. Those individual connections are called neural pathways, and they are the real substance of what your brain does for you. Each neural pathway corresponds with a thought pattern and/or a behavior. If you're trying to do the math on how many neural pathways you'd have, let us help. the correct calculation would be 100,000,000,000 to the 100,000,000,000th power, which is essentially a 1 followed by so many zeroes it would take four years to write all of them. It may as well be "infinity." The key to understand here is that the neural pathways involved in your *sub*conscious processing outnumber those involved in your conscious processing by about 1,000,000 to 1. For every thought or behavior that you are aware of, there's a *gigantic* number that you are unaware of. And it's the part that you're unaware of that actually gets you the results.

One of the books that's influenced our company and our clients the most is a book called *The Ant and the Elephant*, by Vince Poscente. We highly recommend that you buy and read this book – it's tremendous and also very simple. Our Cliff's Notes version of it is super helpful in understanding the exponential difference in horsepower between your conscious and subconscious, so we'll give it to you here.

* * *

The basic narrative starts with this ant. This ant is unhappy with his situation in life – works all the time, never has enough, works all the time, barely getting by, works all the time, you get the picture. Classic "ant life," right? This particular ant is also haunted by the feeling that there's a much more meaningful and abundant life that he was meant for, but he just can't quite grasp it.

Enter the owl. The wise old owl hears the ant grumbling about his life and hoots, "Hey, friend, you seem a little frustrated."

Ant: "Yeah, I am a little frustrated! I work all the time, barely get by, and I feel like I was meant for so much more."

Owl: "That's because you *were* meant for so much more. And guess what? You can be/do/have all of that, but you've got to get to the oasis."

Ant: "The Oasis? I thought that was just a myth . . . it's actually a real place?"

Owl: "Absolutely real, and you need to get there. Better news – you *can* get there, it's not even that far away. From here, the Oasis is due east."

Ant: "Great! How do I get there? Can we go now?!"

Owl: "Well . . . here's your problem, Mr. Ant. You can't see this because of your Ant perspective, but the real issue here is that *you live on the back of an elephant.* And the bad news is that this elephant you live on is currently walking west.

> You can 'go-go-go' all you want, but unless you get this elephant turned around, you'll never get there."

* * *

You may have figured this out, but this fable actually is a totally accurate way of understanding the relationship between your conscious brain (the Ant) and your subconscious (the Elephant). For those of you who are like us, whose brains get a little addled by numbers like "a hundred billion to the hundred billionth power," talking animals might be a little easier to grasp.

The real reason why we experience running hard but not getting anywhere is that we're trying to use our Ant to do an Elephant's job!

Now before you start thinking *Well, I guess I'm doomed. Clearly my Elephant is walking the wrong direction, so I'll never get to my Oasis,* hold on for a second. You absolutely can get there, you just have to know how to talk to your Elephant. When you learn how to communicate with your subconscious in the way it actually responds to, you can definitely get that big beast moving in the right direction, and you know what happens when you do that?

It becomes almost impossible to fail. If you've got your Elephant moving in the right direction, your Ant can literally screw up almost everything else and you'll still get to the oasis. The rest of this section is all about how to communicate with that Elephant, and it starts with understanding its language.

Difference #2: Your Elephant Literally Speaks a Different Language from Your Ant – You Need to Speak *Both* Languages

Your conscious brain operates in logic, reason, evaluating and deciding. It understands time, consequences, and if/then thinking. Your subconscious runs on a different premise entirely. The two parts of your brain literally speak different languages.

And it's important to understand just how different these languages are. You know how some languages are alike enough that if you speak one you're pretty close to speaking the other? Like if you speak French, you actually have a pretty good start on Italian or Spanish? The language barrier between the two parts of your brain is not like that. It's more like the difference between French and German. French and German are totally different in every way – vocabulary, grammar rules, sentence structure, everything, right? If you speak French and assume that means you're good at German, that assumption will be false, and make you look foolish. Sure, France and Germany border each other on the map, but the languages may as well come from different planets. If you think your understanding of one gives you insight into the other, that will cause you problems, right?

Same goes for the different languages of your Ant and your Elephant. Being really good at using your Ant would make you good at Ant things.

- Intellectual
- Book smart
- Logical
- Driven

You'd also be good with a number of other things that we in the business world tend to value. To be clear, these are all very positive characteristics (especially as a foundation for success), but they do not translate to the tools necessary for quantum leaps or effortless (and therefore sustainable) performance. Quantum leaps and effortless performance require the ability to *let go* and tap into:

- Intuition
- Gut feel
- Creativity
- A sense of natural timing

All of these elements of success reside in your subconscious. They are your Elephant's domain alone. So if you want to experience quantum leaps, breakthroughs, and a more elegant path to results, pay attention and understand this:

The language of your subconscious is *pictures.*

The Power of a Mental Image

Your subconscious brain – that big Elephant who does all of your moving forward – *thinks purely in pictures.* Whereas your conscious brain uses thoughts, words, and logical coherent "thoughts," your subconscious is the opposite. It's completely visual and emotional. In fact, it's maybe the best way to understand what your subconscious fundamentally does.

Your subconscious Elephant simply sees a destination and moves toward it. That's all.

It's very powerful, it's very strong, and it's very fast, but it can't evaluate. When it latches onto a clear picture of a destination, your subconscious doesn't decide if it's a good destination or a bad destination. It just moves toward that destination.

Another way of understanding this as it shows up in your behavior is that *your subconscious will simply see a picture and then cause you to act like that picture is real . . . even if it's not.*

You may have heard it said that your mind can't tell the difference between reality and a vividly imagined picture – this is true, especially for your subconscious. If you can picture something vividly enough, your Elephant will actually take it as truth, and will then cause you to act like the picture is your reality.

There's a fairly well-known example of this phenomenon, taught by many great coaches over the past few decades. You can do it while you're reading this. . . .

The Reality of a Fake Lemon

As vividly as you can in your mind, just picture a lemon. Can you see it? Bright yellow, kind of shiny, oblong in shape. Good. In your mind's eye, cut that lemon in half. Now look at the inside – see the little pie-shaped segments and the seeds? Good work.

Now hold that lemon up to your nose and smell. You get that good, clean, lemony smell? Nice. Now open your mouth, shove that half of the lemon in your mouth and *bite* it. . . .

Pause for a moment and notice what's happening with your body. Right now as you're reading, we bet your mouth is full of saliva, the sides of your jaw probably sting a bit, your face and shoulders are tense and you may even have a full "pucker-face." True?

See, this goofy little exercise is a perfect example of the interaction between your conscious and subconscious brain. You conjured up the image of that lemon intentionally and consciously – you used your "Ant" to do it. Once that picture became clear in your mind, your subconscious Elephant (which governs *all* of your body's automatic processes without you paying any attention) took over, and it physically caused your body to react as if that lemon really went into your mouth. Weird, we know – but the implications are far reaching.

Take Time to Visualize the Specific Outcome

You'll learn more about the ridiculous power of clarity in Chapter 7, but let's start to understand here that *this* is why it's so critical to be able to see your objectives clearly. Just giving your Elephant a mental picture of what you want makes you so much more likely to realize it.

You may realize that elite athletes use this principle all the time. If you observe a professional golfer, a basketball player, an Olympic gymnast or runner or figure skater, you will see that they *visualize* their outcomes before they achieve them. It's one of the very best uses of the "slow down to go faster" concept that you'll ever see. Right before performing, a great athlete won't just slow down, they'll actually completely stop and do nothing other than focus their mind on a very specific mental picture of the exact outcome they're looking for. They picture it. The subconscious can then absorb that picture and make it real.

So it's no coincidence that great leaders, great sales professionals, and great businesspeople use the same process. Before they perform, they *visualize* success. Before beginning a week, a day, a meeting, a presentation, or any situation where their performance will determine a significant result, they invest time to *stop* and see clearly in their mind the results they want to achieve, then they let their subconscious find the most elegant path.

Clarity Is King

Here's the most critical application of this principle: *Upgrade your clarity*.

Get clearer about

#1 What You Want and

#2 Why You Want That

If you'll just do this one thing for yourself – *upgrade your clarity* about what you want and why you want it – this one huge key can unlocks the enormous potential of your subconscious. As one of my greatest teachers, Janet Attwood, is so fond of saying, "When you're clear, what you want will show up . . . but only to the degree that you're clear." In fact, this clarity issue is such a big deal for your brain, it's one of the first places where a good coach can really be worth the investment.

Again, more in Chapter 7 about how to generate some "clarity upgrades" in your specific world – for now, let's uncover the second key to understanding your subconscious. Specifically, let's learn what your Elephant does *not* understand.

Difference #3: Your Subconscious Doesn't Register the Word "No"

Your Subconscious Elephant literally doesn't register the word "no." It's not that it doesn't understand it, the word "no" (or "not" or any contraction involving the words "no" or "not") simply doesn't even register on the subconscious brain. Again, all your subconscious can do is see a picture and move toward it . . . and your subconscious can't register a "not-picture".

Your Brain Is Like a Preschooler

Here's an example of what the subconscious does with a negative instruction, one involving "no," "not," and so forth:

Think about a toddler or preschooler in your life, past or present, a kid somewhere between age of like 3 and 6. Perhaps you've got kids or grandkids of this age – if so, you're probably experiencing this phenomenon regularly. Perhaps you used to have kids this age and you remember this occurring.

If you've ever told a child of that age *not* to do something, what did they do almost immediately? Exactly the thing you just told them *not* to do, right?

- You said, "Hey buddy, don't run out in the street," and what happened immediately? The kid's running out in the street!
- You said, "Don't spill your milk." And the next thing you know, the milk is all over the place.
- And so on . . .

If you don't understand why this happens so frequently, it's super frustrating as a parent, right?

From Roger: I can tell you that it was *extremely* frustrating for me – it always felt like our children were intentionally defying me just to push my buttons, but that's just not the case. Understanding the why behind this phenomenon can remove all kinds of anger and stress, especially when you understand that it applies to you, too.

The reason that kids 6 and under so often do exactly what you just told them not to do, is that *they have only a subconscious brain.* The part of the brain that governs conscious thinking doesn't really start developing in a human until around age 7. So kids 6 and under literally don't have an Ant – they operate purely on the principles of the Elephant. This means that logic, common sense, if/then thinking, and reasoning are simply not part of the equation for them yet. This is not a bad thing . . . It's a big part of why kids that age are so awesome! It's why they're totally uninhibited, why they're so visual, why they like to draw, why they're so creative and have such incredible imaginations. On the flip side, it's also why they often have wild mood swings for no apparent reason, why they throw tantrums, why they can't see further than 30 seconds into the future. There are strong plusses and minuses that we'll talk about how to harness . . . for now just understand that the little kid you've been thinking of here has only a subconscious, and the subconscious simply doesn't hear the word "no" in any form.

So when you tell a kid "don't run out in the street," what's that little Elephant actually hearing? Right . . . "Run out in the street!" Elephant sees that picture and BANG, out in the street he goes. It's important to note that when this happens, it's not a failing of the kid: As far as his little brain knows, he is just following the instructions given.

What to Do with a Preschooler?

You've likely realized this in the last few minutes: the key in this situation is that instead of telling the kid what *not* to do, you just have to tell him what *to* do. Instead of "Don't run out in the street," what works much better is "Hey, stay in the yard." Because of the nonrelationship to the word "no," positive instructions just work w-a-a-a-y-y-y better than negative ones.

Why are we spending this much space talking about little kids? It's because fundamentally, *you operate just like that kid.*

You still have that Elephant running the show all day and night, and your elephant still can't register the word "no." The only real difference between you and that preschooler is that now you are grown up and you've got a conscious "Ant" that you can use to make decisions, use logic, and see potential consequences. But that Ant still rides on the back of that Elephant, and that Elephant does not hear the word no. It only receives input, sees pictures, and *moves.*

What to Do with You?

You've got to stop focusing on what you don't want. Stop wallowing, stop worrying, stop obsessing over what you are trying to avoid, because your worrying, wallowing and obsessing is actually making you way more likely to get exactly what you want to avoid.

Think about it – your subconscious

- Has *all* the horsepower
- Sees pictures (without judgment), and makes you act like they're real
- Doesn't register the word "no"

So if you've ever had a conversation (like the ones we have fairly often with our coaching clients) and you said something like, "Yeah, I know what I'm shooting for . . . I don't want to be broke (or sick, or stressed out, or angry, or failing, or whatever)!" . . . consider how your subconscious received that message and how your subconscious responded.

You said, "I don't want to be broke."

Your Elephant *heard*, "I want to be broke."

And then all it could do was create a picture of – you guessed it – you going *broke*. And it started making that picture real, even if it wasn't.

That's how focusing on, obsessing over, and worrying about what you *don't* want actually draws more of it into your life. When it comes to achieving your goals, your *main job* is to keep your Elephant pointed in the right direction. This is done when you stop focusing on what you *don't* want, and start focusing more on what you *do* want. Just like your kid does way better when you tell him what *to* do, your brain does way better when you focus it on what you *do* want.

Unseeing Isn't an Option

And here's a helpful key: Your subconscious Elephant can't cancel or "unsee" a picture once it's seen it . . . but it can *replace* a picture pretty quickly. You may have done part of this next little exercise before (it's pretty common among speakers and coaches like us), but just try to follow the instructions we're about to give.

Right now, *do not* think of a pink elephant. Of course, what just immediately popped into your mind? *Pink elephant.*

Okay, now, *do not* think of a blue monkey.

So let's look at this: If you observe your mind right now, what's there? A blue monkey, right? Just that quickly, you replaced the pink elephant with a blue monkey. You couldn't just un-see the pink elephant . . . if you had sat there pounding your head and shouting "Stop it, stop it, stop it!" you'd still be looking at that pink elephant.

But you can replace a picture quite easily. Just by hearing us ask you about a blue monkey, now that's what your mind is looking at.

And the same is true with less cartoonish things, such as your goals. When your mind gets locked on problems, failures, worry, and what you *don't* want, you draw more of them into your life and it doesn't feel good. But it just takes a pause, a breath, and a gentle reminding yourself of your picture of what you *do* want in order to get back on track, and quickly begin the opposite process, one that works and feels much better. If you can get your mind focused on seeing that "Oasis," you'll change the direction of your Elephant's movement, starting immediately. When you're clear about what you want, what you want will show up – but only to the degree that you're clear.

Difference #4: Your Subconscious Already Knows "How"

The last thing to know about your subconscious Elephant is that it already knows *how*. When you decide what you want, there's this weird dynamic where your subconscious knows the best path to get you there instinctively. It also knows instinctively how to navigate the obstacles that pop up along the way, exactly like a real live elephant.

Imagine for a moment that you're physically riding on a real live elephant. You and your elephant are physically walking down a trail through the jungle, and you're on your way to an oasis. Just before a curve in the trail, you notice that a big tree has fallen across the path, blocking your progress. Got the picture?

We'll suggest that you do not need to know what to do with this tree *because your elephant knows instinctively what to do*. You don't need to issue a single instruction, your elephant just *knows*. In the blink of an eye, he goes through the options:

- Do I walk around this tree?
- Do I step over this tree?
- Do I lift this tree with my super powerful trunk and move it out of the way?
- Do I stop for a moment and *eat* this tree?

And then instantly *knows* which one works best. That's what instinct does for a real live elephant. And again, this is exactly what your subconscious does, too. To harness that power, one of your main jobs is just to *get out of the way*. Here's why:

If you've ever experienced serendipity – a wonderful coincidence that just seemed like magic – that was your subconscious leading you there.

If you've ever said or done the exact right thing in a presentation, the thing that closed the deal almost like magic, and when you asked "where did *that* come from?" well, that was your subconscious giving you the words and the actions.

If you've ever been on such a roll that money and results seemed to effortlessly flow to you from both known and unknown sources – you simply couldn't make a mistake – that was your subconscious keeping your Money Magnet turned on.

We could go on and on, but you get the idea. In any of these situations you experienced that feeling of Flow, or of being "In The Zone." That's a feeling that comes with a lot of great energy *and* a profound sense of calm ease. You can't get that kind of mojo with your conscious brain – that's not your Ant's job. That kind of mojo has to come from your subconscious. . . .

And one of the primary things that prevents this, is getting too wrapped up in the *how*. Devoting too much thought to what teacher Michael Dooley calls the "cursed hows" will literally cripple your creativity and also cause you much stress in the process.

You Can Let Go of "How"

Let's go back to you and your elephant, walking through the jungle, arriving at that tree that fell over. Multiple-choice quiz: If your elephant knows what to do instinctively in this situation and is perfectly equipped to handle it, what do *you* need to do to best help?

A. Fret over the size of the tree and wail about how you'll never get around it.

B. Give the elephant detailed instructions on how to get around the tree.

C. Give the elephant a motivational speech to make him feel more strong and powerful.

D. Post a picture of this tree on Facebook to see if your friends have "suggestions" on how to get around a tree, except really your post is just a poorly concealed plea for affirmation that trees suck, and furthermore your life is so hard.

E. None of the above: Simply relax, appreciate the majesty of nature, and let the elephant get you past the tree with zero effort on your part.

Okay, this may seem a little obvious, but seriously, think about this. A is clearly a nonstarter for anyone reading a book like this, probably D is too, but wow do people resort to these two a lot. If you're doing either of these at all, it's just not helpful.

Answer B actually sounds like it might be helpful (especially to a manager or an engineer), but you have to remember that the elephant already knows what to do. That means that any amount of instruction *you* provide is

- A total waste of energy
- Probably really annoying the elephant

Answer C is similar to B in its non-necessity, though it might make the Elephant chuckle a little.

If you chose E, you win! In this example, literally the only thing you need to do is just trust the elephant to do what's right. Repeat after us: *You must trust your elephant.*

In the same way, you must learn to trust your subconscious. It's *hugely* powerful, focused like a laser-guided missile on your destination, and it's connected on the deepest levels to every resource you need. Stop spazzing over "How am I supposed to get there?", and get way more dialed in to "Where am I trying to go?" and "Why do I want to get there in the first place?"

What versus Why versus How

If you've read Simon Sinek's outstanding book *Start with Why*, you've likely seen something like the model in Figure 2.1.

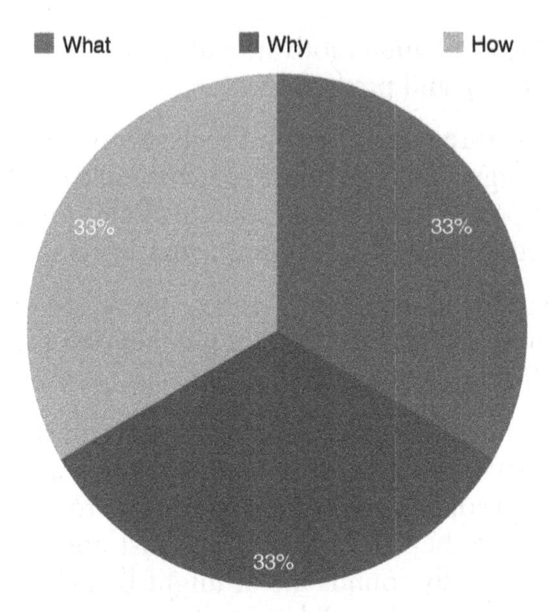

Figure 2.1 The What, Why, How Model

Sinek does an incredible job of talking about how great leaders "Start with Why," as in *Why* does our organization do what it does, then they focus on *How* we execute, and then finally on *What* we want to accomplish. It's an awesome model for leaders and for organizations, and we highly recommend his book for anyone interested in leadership.

When it comes to your own personal performance and specifically helping your subconscious to get you massive results quickly, let's look at this model slightly differently.

From your brain's perspective, whenever you want to achieve a certain result, there's fundamentally three places where your thought energy can be directed.

1. *What* do I want to accomplish?
2. *Why* do I want to accomplish that?
3. *How* do I accomplish it?

The pie chart lays it out as if each of these three questions gets equal billing, but that's deceptive. Nobody ever gives What, Why, and How exactly one third of their thought energy, nor should they. Every single human being will give a disproportionate amount of energy to one of these three, and this indicates a key difference between top performers and "The Majority".

(Please recall that "The Majority" almost always has it backwards, which is a major reason why they struggle so much with everything from money to health to relationships and so on.)

The majority of the population will devote 80–90 percent to either thinking or straight-up worrying about How, which leaves only 10–20 percent to be split between What and Why. This would look like Figure 2.2.

Consider how this would feel, with 90 percent of your thoughts wrapped up in How. When our clients look at this chart and really absorb the implications, they realize that this level of obsession with How is, well, exhausting. When combined with the almost total lack of thought toward "What do I want in the first place?" and "Why do I want that?," this mix becomes not only stressful and tiring, but creates a deep disconnect with meaning and purpose. It's truly a recipe for burnout and giving up.

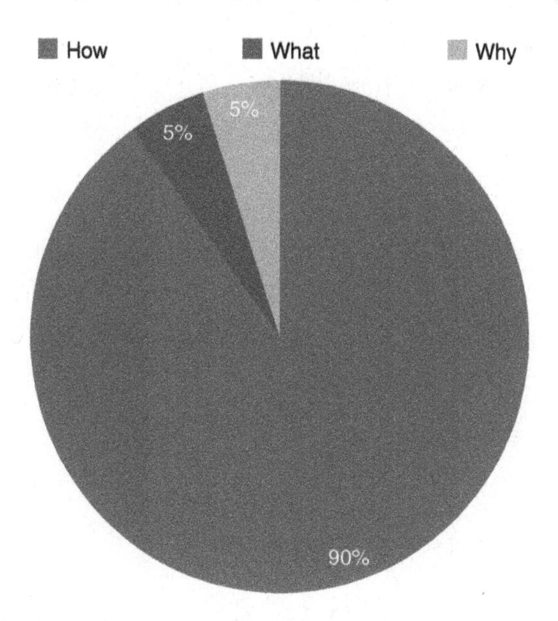

Figure 2.2 Most People Focus on How, Leaving Little Space for What and Why

Top performers in every field show a strong tendency not to try and balance these ratios. Top performers reverse them. If they're going to obsess about something (which they do a lot), it tends to be about What they want and Why they want it . . . and they often let the How take care of itself. This looks more like Figure 2.3.

Please note: Top Performers *do* focus on How – the chart doesn't show zero percent in this area. Some level of planning, strategizing, and implementing tactics is in fact part of the mix. In fact, one characteristic of Top Performers is a high level of mastery over their tactics. They have a really good How, it's just not what they obsess over and dream about. Top performers let the How take care of itself, to a much greater extent than The Majority, and it's a big part of what makes them Top Performers.

Now this might be counterintuitive, but it completely makes sense if you think about it from the perspective of your subconscious. Connecting with What you want (a.k.a. where you're going) provides clarity and guidance. Connecting with Why provides fuel, perseverance, grit, and intestinal fortitude.

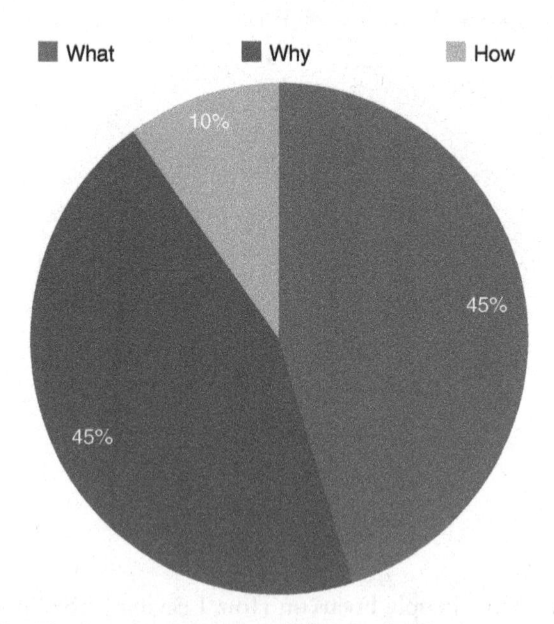

Figure 2.3 Top Leaders Focus on What and Why

The How needs to be addressed, but the thing is that once you've been trained and have some patterns down (which doesn't take that long), the How can take care of itself pretty naturally.

Call it intuition, call it guts, call it what you will, but your subconscious always knows how and it always knew how. It doesn't need a lot of help figuring out the best way to do things. It knows how to set a meeting. It knows how to pick up the phone. It knows how to write a proposal. It knows how to place an implant. It knows how to deliver a presentation. What your brain actually needs is clarity on why it is important to be doing whatever it is you want it to do in the first place.

Let's go back one more time to our elephant in the jungle at the tree. In navigating the obstacle, the elephant would actually not even need to stop and think about what to do. It would not ask around for advice on how to mitigate the situation. It would not be paralyzed by indecisiveness. It would simply step over the obstacle or move it with its trunk or walk around it, no questions asked. This is because the elephant knows what is important: getting to the oasis where it will get a treat.

We work with a lot of people who for years (and decades) have been told that taking action and "doing" their job is the most important thing they can do to get results. They come to us because that mindset, that approach is *not* getting them the results they want. One of the most effective ways to get things to work for you instead of against you is to reallocate your mental bandwidth *away* from How stuff and *toward* What stuff and Why stuff.

This "Why" talk is not new. And to be clear, we 100 percent subscribe to and believe in the concept. Once again, Simon Sinek writes:

> The most successful people and most successful organizations focus on WHY they do what they do, not how or what they do.

But how you move away from How and toward What and Why isn't simple. It doesn't happen automatically. The good news is that once you figure out how to reallocate that mental bandwidth, results, success, wins, and excitement start to happen *rapidly*. Here's an example of what happens when you move from How and What to Why.

A Case Study in How versus Why: Dane Johnston

Dane came to us as a successful financial planner and promising entrepreneur in the outdoor world. He had built a successful financial planning business and the profits from that business had allowed him to build a dream home on a large piece of land and start a hobby business around his passion, fishing. In this hobby business, Dane had brought a few products to market in the fishing space that had proven to be great, differentiating, and highly successful. He also had ideas for either manufacturing or licensing a half dozen other products in the space. To date, he had sold a bunch of products and was revenue positive. As a result, he had set an aggressive, but manageable, five-year revenue goal for that business. But then the business stalled out as a result of his activity level and he was kind of stuck.

On our first call, Dane shared with me that he didn't feel like planning/time management was his weakness. He was very clear in his head on what he wanted to work on and how much time he wanted to dedicate to each task. As a matter of fact, Dane sent me his planning process, which was six cross-linked spreadsheets detailing *everything*. I saw columns and rows of data. He had listed five-year goals, one-year goals, tasks he felt needed to be accomplished, his leading activities, lagging activities, and the amount of time he was planning on spending on these activities on a daily, weekly, and monthly basis. About the only thing that wasn't accounted for was eating, sleeping, and going to the bathroom. When he asked me what I thought of his process and how thorough he was, my only response was, "Well, Dane, I think you have successfully engineered the bejeezus out of your life!" We had a good laugh about that, and then I was pleasantly surprised by his response:

"That's kinda the way I've always done it. It seems to be working, but do you think I'm overthinking things? Because sometimes I feel like I'm too methodical, and even though I have everything listed out with regard to what I need to accomplish, I just don't know where to start."

"Ummm, yeah. I think you are overthinking things. And over-planning things and over-"what"ing things and over-"how"ing things, and, most important, just overdoing things"

This ended up becoming a springboard for the best conversation about the whole How/What/Why thing I've ever been a part of. Here's the Cliff's Notes on that conversation.

* * *

Dane needed to "flip the script" on his approach. He was super focused on what to do and how to do it, but lacked any real clarity on why he was doing what he was doing in the first place.

This was a big challenge for him. After all, because of his success "building plans" for his clients in the financial services world, there wasn't any reason the same approach shouldn't be applied to his own life. But that's where the disconnect started. By focusing on the small day-to-day tasks, he became overly focused on small day-to-day tasks. Those tasks kept adding up and adding up and eventually, he had to wade through a mess of piddly little decisions in order to get to the point where he could make a larger decision. As a result, big decisions never got made and his tasks often were left unfinished. And, as I'm sure you can deduct, with no tasks being accomplished, progress toward the one-year goal suffered. Work toward the five-year goal? Totally nonexistent.

The biggest thing Dane and I worked on from that point forward was his vision statement. And we spent a *lot* of time on it. Almost three times longer than most folks I work with. We needed to create a vivid image or picture of what he really wanted out of life and why that life was so important to him. In short, we needed a big bucket of Elephant food. So we did just that. We went back to understanding why he worked so hard to build his house and his pond and improve his property. Turns out, he just wanted a kick-ass pond to fish in and have the opportunity to do what he loved with his kids.

Working backward, we created a picture of what his ideal life would look like. How much was he working? How was he making money? How much vacation was he taking? Where was he going? What did the hobby business do to contribute to his overall quality of life? How much time was he spending there versus in his "real" job?

Once we had it nailed down, Dane had one piece of homework: Read his vision statement every day, twice a day, and practice visualizing living that life like it was happening *now*. He was instructed to "Act like you have done this before" and make decisions like he already had everything he wanted.

This went on for a few months, while we were working on some other projects together. And then one day, about six months later, we hopped on our call and I'll never forget the first words out of his mouth.

"So this is weird . . . Everything just got *really* easy. Everything I need to make a decision on, the right decision is always easy to find and it always makes me a lot of money. All the stuff I need to get done to hit my goals is just really easy to accomplish, almost like I don't have to put any effort in. Mostly because I keep ending up in these situations where the only right course of action *totally* works in my favor and gets me the result I want. I think my Elephant just figured stuff out . . . and I *like* it!"

Jackpot.

The thing is, his Elephant didn't just "figure stuff out." His Elephant knew what to do the whole time. He just needed to get all the small How and What items out of the way so that the Elephant could get to where it wanted to go faster. Spreadsheets and rows and columns and times and dates and numbers, while important, were actually holding him back. Once he got away from focusing on that type of information and instead focused on gaining clarity on the big picture, everything moved a lot faster for him.

Using the driving-in-the-snow analogy again, remember that the first car following the plow has the best path. Be the plow and clear a path for your Elephant by minimizing the How and What stuff, and you'll be amazed at how quickly your results can appear. And sometimes they appear in the unlikeliest of places!

Chapter Review

- Your subconscious brain differs from your conscious brain in four ways:
  1. It's *orders of magnitude* larger than your conscious brain.
  2. It thinks in pictures.
  3. It doesn't register *no*.
  4. It already knows How.
- Spend lots less time focusing on the How and What and reallocate your energy to clarify Why what you are doing is important to you.
- Connecting with Why ideas keeps your Elephant (subconscious brain) moving in the right direction.

3

Understanding and Harnessing Your Brain Wave Patterns

Your brain is vibrating.

I'm not saying this as a warning to help you avoid embarrassment, like when someone says "hey, you've got some broccoli in your teeth," or "yo, your fly is open." I'm just telling you that whether you know it or not, your brain is vibrating all the time, just like everything else in the universe, and *how* it's vibrating is having a gigantic impact on your results and your enjoyment of your life. Understanding and influencing how your brain is vibrating is also where the rubber meets the road in terms of slo-o-o-wing down in order to get results faster. Learning how and when to literally slow down and deepen the vibrational frequency of your brain is the most effective way to attract abundance and productivity to our worlds and those of our clients. We will be getting a little science-y here, but check this out. . . .

One of the more profoundly helpful discoveries of the last century is that your brain is both a transmitter and a receiver of electromagnetic vibration,very similar to a radio. It can be "tuned in" to both receive and broadcast different frequencies, and just as with a radio, at different frequencies you will experience different things? When you're in Madison, Wisconsin, and you tune your radio to 100.3 FM, you experience sports-talk radio. Tune into 101.5 FM and you get classic rock. Different frequencies get you different experiences – your radio picks up what's being broadcast on the frequency you've tuned into and feeds it back to you verbatim. The radio doesn't judge what's being broadcast, it just gives it to you.

Same goes for your brain. Whatever it's "tuned into" is what it will give you. The tactics and strategies you'll learn in Part II are all essentially different approaches guaranteed to tune your brain to the more helpful frequencies, so you experience the more helpful outcomes. So again, we do recommend that you read this chapter for foundational understanding (our clients usually really enjoy learning this stuff), but if you feel an urgent need to jump directly to tactics and skip the science, feel free to go directly to Part II.

Applying the Very Real Hippie-Dippy-Woo-Woo Law of Attraction

So you're sticking around for this chapter . . . we applaud you . . . but right now we need to take a bit of a side trip into some territory that will strike different readers differently. If you're a conservative/analytical/business type, the next few pages may seem a little touchy-feely, hippie-dippy woo-woo at first, but please hang with us. We're both results-oriented businessmen, and we promise this stuff shows up on the bottom line. That practicality is actually a big reason why our top-producer coaching clients stick with us for years and years.

If you're already a touchy-feely, hippie-dippy woo-woo type, you've likely already studied some of this and you'll love the next few pages.

Regardless of where you're coming from you'll find value if you pay close attention as we nerd out at some of the places where science, spirituality and straight-up profits all blend together. . . .

On a metaphysical level, what you're about to learn here is definitely involved with the principle of *sympathetic resonance*, and in turn what many refer to as the Law of Attraction. A brief primer on both follows.

Sympathetic (or harmonic) resonance is just the principle that when one thing is vibrating strongly enough at a certain frequency, it'll cause certain other things to vibrate or resonate at the same frequency. The principle is easily illustrated with sound vibrations: If you strike a C note on a piano, that sound broadcasts through the room, and a tuning fork across the room that's been tuned to C will start vibrating and playing the same note, seemingly on its own. It seems like magic, but it's not. It's just Sympathetic Resonance.

The Law of Attraction is the human version of this principle. On the subatomic level, every person including you is vibrating at a specific frequency, and that frequency literally "broadcasts." Some would say it broadcasts infinitely, but we don't even need to go there. For our purposes here, let's just understand that anything that comes in contact with your vibration and is "tuned" to the same frequency . . . will resonate at that same frequency. What makes this unique in the human experience is that when something resonates with your frequency, it will *move toward you.* Things like money, circumstances, people, and coincidences start showing up in your world in alignment with whatever you and your mind are vibrating and broadcasting out to the world. That's the Law of Attraction in a nutshell.

What we're saying here is that *if you change your vibration, you will change your results, and it can't be any other way.* Ever wonder why people who complain a lot seem to legitimately have so much to complain about? Or why other people just seem to be "lucky?" The reason has a lot to do with Sympathetic Resonance.

Everything, material and ephemeral, carries a vibrational frequency. Money has a frequency. People have a frequency. All emotions, positive or negative, have a frequency. Organizational cultures have a frequency. And when things vibrate at a certain frequency, they are

(*continued*)

(*continued*)

magnetized toward anything else that vibrates at that same frequency. This is not our opinion, it's physics. So if you're "vibrating negative," you'll inevitably draw more negative into your life. If you start "vibrating positive" more often, you'll draw more positive into your life.

And even if you're the most staunchly conservative/analytical/business person on the planet, you'll see this principle showing up in lots of places. You've heard that "like attracts like," right? That "birds of a feather flock together"? And if you look back on your life, specifically at times when you encountered the exact right person at the exact right time to make something incredible happen, you'll likely recall that you were in a state of both high energy and clarity. If that's ever happened to you, it's the classic example of the principles of sympathetic resonance and the Law of Attraction just doing what they do. Those principles can be intentionally harnessed, and an upgraded understanding of brain wave patterns and frequencies is a great place to start.

(If you'd like to study more well-rounded studies on the science and practical application of Sympathetic Resonance and the Law of Attraction, there are plenty to read. We'd recommend starting with Napoleon Hill's *Think and Grow Rich*, John Assaraf's *The Answer*, and David Hawkins' *Power vs. Force.* If you'd like to have your mind blown by science, check out the work of Dr. Masaru Emoto and his *Hidden Messages in Water*, which is featured in the movie *What the Bleep Do We Know?*)

The Fraternity of Beta Alpha Theta Delta

Much of the earliest information about brain wave patterns as measured by frequency, amplitude, and their effect on our lives was disseminated by Ned Herrmann. Ned Herrmann is an educator who has developed models of brain activity and integrated them into teaching and management training. Before founding the Ned Herrmann Group in 1980, he headed management education at General Electric, where he developed many of his ideas. Here is his explanation, excerpted from Mr. Herrmann's book *The Creative Brain:*

> Electrical activity emanating from the brain is displayed in the form of brainwaves. There are four categories of these brainwaves, ranging from the most activity to the least activity. When the brain is aroused and actively engaged in mental activities, it generates beta waves. The frequency of beta waves ranges from 15 to 40 cycles a second. Beta waves are characteristics of a strongly engaged mind. A person in active conversation would be in beta. A person making a speech, or a teacher, or a talk show host would all be in beta.
>
> The next brainwave category in order of frequency is alpha. Where beta represented arousal, alpha represents non-arousal. Their frequency ranges from 9 to 14 cycles per second. A person who takes time out to reflect or meditate is usually in an alpha state.
>
> The next state, theta brainwaves, are of even greater amplitude and slower frequency. This frequency range is normally between 5 and 8 cycles a second. A person who has taken time off from a task and begins to daydream is often in a theta brainwave state.
>
> Individuals who run outdoors often are in theta and when in theta, they are prone to a flow of ideas. The ideation during the theta state is often free flow and occurs without censorship or guilt. It is typically a very positive mental state.
>
> The final brainwave state is delta. Here the brainwaves are of the greatest amplitude and slowest frequency. They never go down to zero . . . But, deep dreamless sleep would take you down to the lowest frequency.
>
> When an individual awakes from a deep sleep in preparation for getting up, their brainwave frequencies will increase through the different specific stages of brainwave activity. That is, they will increase from delta to theta and then to alpha and finally, when the

> alarm goes off, into beta. During this awakening cycle it is possible for individuals to stay in the theta state for an extended period of say, five to 15 minutes – which would allow them to have a free flow of ideas about yesterday's events or to contemplate the activities of the forthcoming day. This time can be an extremely productive.

Now that was from a book written in 1989, but it helps us understand a lot about why we operate the way we do. Here's an updated take on what that just said (more research has been done since 1989), along with some action steps:

You have four predominant brain wave states: beta, alpha, theta, and delta (see Figure 3.1). Interestingly enough, these are laid out from fastest to slowest, and you'll see that intentionally tapping in and programming in the slower brain wave states is where you can make the biggest quantum leaps forward.

Beta: The "Awake" State

Beta is the highest frequency (i.e., the fastest) brain wave pattern, but has the lowest amplitude (least forceful). Since we're talking

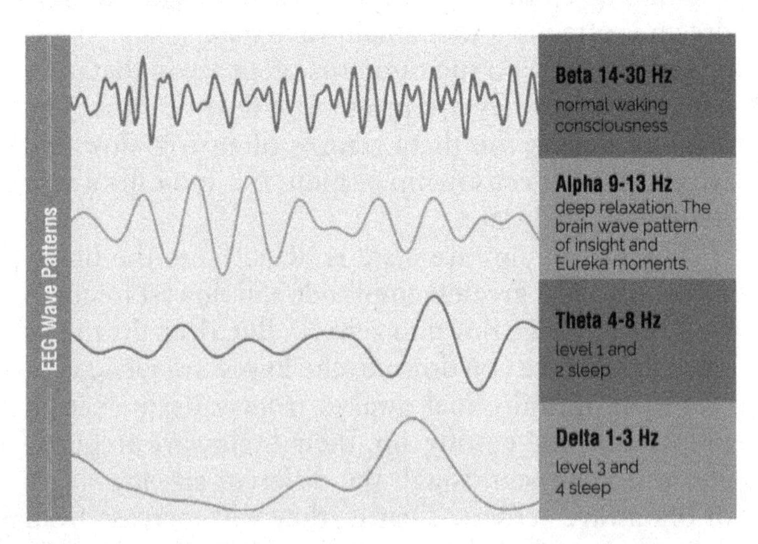

Figure 3.1 The Four Types of Human Brain Waves

about waves here, it's helpful to visualize waves on the water. If you're standing by a pond and a light breeze blows across it, you'll get small ripples. You'd notice that those ripples lap up on the shore in rapid succession (with high frequency), but no individual wave would carry much force (low amplitude).

Beta brain waves are associated with lots of good things: alertness, problem solving, logic, and, as Herrmann says, "high states of arousal." The beta state is where you do most of your conscious thinking. For example, your Ant is all about beta brain waves.

Truthfully, there's not a whole lot we need to teach you about how to maximize your beta state, because you're likely already doing it. Beta is actually predominant through most of your waking hours . . . it's just how you go about your day.

Alpha: The "Relaxed" State

The alpha brain wave state is a little lower frequency (i.e., slower), but you'll notice it has higher amplitude (more forceful). Going back to our water analogy, these would be like when there's a stiff breeze blowing across a large lake, creating two- to three-foot whitecapped waves.

Alpha is a super important state to understand, because alpha is strongly associated with memory, with recall, and with learning. Your brain remembers better when you're in alpha, it recalls better in alpha, and so you do your best learning when you're in alpha.

When does alpha happen? It happens when you're *relaxed* – the main indicator of an alpha state is that you are both mentally and physically deeply relaxed. You can induce an alpha state for short periods (more on how to do that in a bit), but your brain will naturally be in an alpha pattern twice a day: shortly after you wake up, and shortly before you go to sleep at night.

The specific amount of time will vary from person to person and from day to day, but the general rule is that you've got a lot of alpha going on for the first 15–20 minutes after you wake up in the morning. You know that period where you're technically awake, probably even up and moving, but you're not quite all there yet? Body's a little stiff, mind is still a little groggy . . . mentally and physically, you're still "warming up" to the day. That's alpha state.

This warming-up period is wildly important for your day, because everything that goes into your mind in this state, you remember whether you want to or not. It tends to stick with you all day, so input during this alpha time impacts your productivity.

The other key "alpha time" in your day is the *last* 10–20 minutes that you're up at night. I know sometimes it feels like you can go from running a million miles an hour directly to face-planting in the pillow (or passing out in front of the TV), but there is a transition period out of your high arousal states and into your sleep. Call it your brain's "cooling down" phase.

This "cooling down" period is also super important, because everything that goes into your mid in this state, you remember whether you want to or not – it tends to stick with you all night, so input during this alpha period impacts your rest, which then impacts your productivity.

If you've ever fallen asleep while watching a scary movie or something stressful (yes, we've all done it), you know how it can give you nightmares and mess with your sleep. That's because of the alpha state – your brain is remembering and processing that input even while you're sleeping. We'll get into some specific strategies to make alpha work for you at the end of this chapter, for now just understand that, during alpha, what goes in stays in whether you want it to or not.

Theta: The "Borderline" State

Theta is where you can create some major impact on your results, with a minuscule investment of focus and time. The theta brain wave state is even lower frequency (slower) than alpha, but even higher amplitude (more forceful). Returning to the water analogy, these waves would be good-sized ocean waves, perfect for surfing.

The key idea is that when you're in a predominantly theta state, you actually have *direct access to your subconscious brain.* This is where your subconscious Elephant is listening closely for instructions, with little or no filtering from your conscious Ant. This is also where your subconscious can deliver to you creative insights and solutions to your problems, as well as cause you to gravitate toward the exact right people and circumstances to achieve your aims. *It's where your subconscious can be most easily guided, and in turn guide you.*

The impact and practical applications of the theta state are incredibly powerful. Many of the greatest leaders and thinkers of our time – Thomas Edison, Albert Einstein, Pablo Picasso, Winston Churchill – had specific, intentional daily practices that allowed them to induce and tap into theta (though they might not have known to call it that). They would do it specifically because their greatest insights and their best creative thinking came from their subconscious brains, and the somewhat hypnotic theta state is the best place to access the subconscious directly.

Again, you'll get some of those practices in the next chapters, but let's learn here that, like alpha, your brain is naturally in a predominantly Theta state twice a day. It happens when you're right on the threshold of sleep and wakefulness. That's right away when you wake up in the morning, and then right as you're falling asleep at night. Again, the specific time frame varies from person to person and day to day, but here's our rule of thumb. You've got a ton of theta for the first two to five minutes you're awake in the morning, and again for the last two to five minutes you're awake at night. It's right when your eyes pop open, and then the last stages of drifting off to sleep.

You'll want to be rigorous about what you allow into your brain during your brief theta periods, *because it sets the tone for either your whole day or your whole night, whether you like it or not.*

Remember how your subconscious doesn't judge what it sees, it just sees it and moves toward it? Nowhere does that show up more powerfully than in the programming that happens right when you wake and right when you're going to sleep. If you wake up with a happy, results-oriented, positive picture, you've set yourself up with a happy, results-oriented, positive day. If you wake up crabby, angry, and fearful, you've set yourself up for a crabby, angry, fearful day. Same thing goes for how you go to sleep – the thoughts you think and the inputs you input as you go to sleep will work on you all night.

So "winning" these transitional theta times will be not simply a good idea – we believe it's the single best investment you can make in your personal development. By best investment, we mean it's when you'll get the biggest return of results for the smallest investment of time and energy. The tactics in Chapter 6, "Programming Your Mind," will help you win these critical minutes of your day.

Delta: The "Deeply Asleep" State

The delta state is the lowest-frequency (slowest) state, but the one with the highest amplitude (most forceful). If you're wondering about the water equivalent, think about surfing on giant ocean waves.

What you want to understand about delta is that it's associated with healing. When your brain drops down into a delta state, it slows wa-a-a-ay down, and this slowdown is key for your health. It's what allows your brain (and your body) to kick off many of its recovery and healing mechanisms. Growth hormone, pituitary hormone, and other key "good drugs" get produced. Much of your brain's processing of the day's learning happens in the delta state. Delta is where memories start to get transferred from short-term to long-term, so it does a lot to cement your learning. In many ways, good quality delta time is the foundation of both your mental and physical health . . . and therefore the foundation of sustainable effectiveness.

You've likely gathered that delta occurs when you're deeply asleep. So there's not a lot we can teach you *to do* in this state, since by definition you're totally unconscious in delta. What we can tell you for sure is that . . .

You.

Need.

Delta!

More specifically, you need to get good sleep, both in quality and quantity. Yes, the correct quantity of sleep will vary from person to person and from season to season (babies and teenagers need a *ton* of sleep, middle-aged folks not so much), so I'm not going to preach a specific number for you. You definitely should, however, experiment and learn what's really right for you, and work to make it happen. There's a huge and growing body of sleep research that shows that

- Getting proper rest is one of the best things you can do for your mood, your productivity, and your longevity.
- Getting insufficient rest is one of the most devastating things that can happen to your mood, your productivity, and your longevity.
- Most people – especially driven, successful, motivated people like you – don't get anywhere near proper rest.

Chapter 6 offers good methods for ensuring proper rest, but for God's sake – you need some delta brain waves, so *get some sleep*!

Chapter Review

- Your brain is vibrating.
- The fraternity of beta alpha theta delta.
- Beta is for being alert.
- Alpha is for learning/memory.
- Theta is for direct access to your subconscious.
- Delta is for healing.

4

Your Brain's Unhelpful Default Settings

A bedrock principle that led us to write this book is that *your mind creates your life*. Largely through the mechanisms that we discuss in this first part, your mind is the single biggest creative driver of your results. The fact that your mind creates your life is a wonderful gift – it's perhaps the biggest gift we're given as human beings!

The thing is, it's a gift that comes with "some assembly required," and some significant problems come right along with it. When we're born, we arrive here with some wiring issues that will cause our brains to work against us. And then as we're raised, these wiring issues get reinforced – so by the time you're even approaching adulthood, we've all developed some default settings that will prevent you from getting where you want to go. If you're not somewhere between proactive and aggressive about working to overcome these default settings, it's virtually guaranteed that they will:

- Stop you from accomplishing your goals.
- Cause turbulence/slow down your progress in every key area of life.
- Add a ton of stress to your life that you definitely don't need.

Not Character Flaws, Just Survival Mechanisms

It's important to note that these default settings are not character flaws. If you notice these in your own life or in people you care for/work with, don't think that these flaws make you or them a bad person. *Everyone* has these tendencies, and each of them is a terrifically effective survival mechanism. Knowing and understanding the ins and outs of these tendencies can help when it comes to understanding how to best interact with others around you; bosses, colleagues, customers, family members, friends, and so forth.

If you live in the wilderness as a hunter/gatherer, these default settings are supremely helpful for keeping you alive. But when it comes to running a business, hitting a goal, or even just being a happy person, these default settings are counterproductive. See if you recognize any of these tendencies in yourself.

Default Setting #1: Your Brain Tends to *Over*emphasize Negative and *Under*emphasize Positive Signals

The first leftover survival mechanism is the wiring that causes us to overemphasize "negative" inputs, and ignore or dismiss the more "positive" inputs. Your brain – whether you knew it or not – is wired to be extremely sensitive to *threats*. So if you live in the wild, this is unbelievably helpful, because there really are threats everywhere! There are grizzly bears, enemy tribes, and all manner of things that want to kill you and/or eat you around every corner. In this situation, the individual who's more sensitive to threats will notice them sooner . . . and therefore is better equipped to deal with those threats so that they survive. If you live in the wilderness, this wiring is critical for your survival.

The problem is that you don't live in the wilderness and you're not under constant threat of death. But you still have this default setting, and it's not helpful. What this wiring does now is to create a number of dynamics that will drain your energy.

The Hidden Costs of Negativity

If you're not working on this default setting proactively, the overemphasis of the negative will cause you to:

- Worry excessively.
- Stress over things that don't need to be stressful.
- Unintentionally view opportunities as threats.
- Repel people who actually like you and/or want to do business with you.
- Live out a vicious cycle of being consistently exhausted and grumpy.

When you get people in groups of two or more humans, this default setting will actually create an entire culture of negativity – it'll steal the smile of a whole office in the blink of an eye. If positive, upbeat energy is important for you getting results, you'll need to be working daily (sometimes even hourly) to overcome this default setting.

Default Setting #2: Your Brain Is Easily (Really Easily) *Consumed* with the Urgent Matter, at the Expense of the Important Matter

Your brain is hard wired to take your focus and divert it to whatever just popped up in front of your face.

Doesn't matter what just popped up, and it really doesn't matter what you were already doing, whatever just floated by is where your attention wants to go. Could be an interruption, phone call, text message, email alert, random thought, or just *squirrel!* Whatever just happened (especially whatever you just saw) is where your focus wants to go. Does this sound familiar?

Again, this reaction comes from a good place – in the wilderness, this default setting is incredibly valuable. We've already established that there are grizzly bears that want to eat you. So if a grizzly bear wants to eat you, specifically *when* does he want to eat you? *Right now!* He's not sending you an Outlook invite or looking to "meet up next week" – you are being attacked right now! Which means that if you don't take action immediately, you will be eaten by a grizzly bear.

This is why your brain has the tendency to be consumed with immediate "threats." Furthermore, you are never asked to make a distinction between "urgent" and "important."

But you don't live in the wilderness, so here's what this default setting does to you now:

Have you ever noticed just how shockingly easily your mind gets distracted and off-track? It's comical when you think about it: you could be at the critical moment in a presentation to a client that, if it goes well, will make you hundreds of thousands of dollars, but if a puppy walks by at that moment? Game over – your brain just left without even an apology.

That example may sound silly, but it's not really that far off. And even if we can joke about distraction for a moment here in these pages, distraction is no joke in your day-to-day life. In fact, distraction can be incredibly expensive. Here's why.

The Insane Cost of Distraction

When you get distracted, an unfair energy drain occurs. Think of a time when you were really focused and then something stole your focus. It required only about a millisecond for your brain to go from "on track" to "off track." But then, how long did it take to return to what you were doing? It required somewhere between 4 and 20 minutes for your brain to fully re-engage at the point where it got off track. Like we said, it's not fair . . . but it is reality.

That time and energy difference can be expensive. Consider how many times per day your mind flies off, and if you believe time is money you can start seeing where this default setting is not a matter of "oh, ha ha, I'm so distracted." Instead, this default setting can wreak havoc on your productivity, undermine your focus, and draw down your energy, your confidence, and your bottom line all day, every day, if you let it.

Default Setting #3: Your Brain Craves Safety, Much More Than You Want "Progress"

If we directly asked you if you'd like to make progress, you'd look at us like we had three heads. Really, what kind of stupid question would that be? You'd say:

"*Of course* I want progress! *Of course* I want to make more this year than last. *Of course* I want to be in better shape. *Of course* I want my kids to have a better life than I did. Why would I even buy this book if I didn't want progress?!"

And you know what? We believe you. We know you want progress, and we want you to make progress, too! Your results are the single best testimonial we can get. Furthermore, we also believe that your family, your coworkers, your community all want you to make progress, because that's how everyone wins together. There's a lot of desire for progress, but that's not your problem.

Your problem is that progress is not what your *brain* wants . . . your brain just wants you to stay where you are. Logically, you want progress, but *bio*logically, your brain craves safety.

Go back to what it would be like if you lived in the wilderness. Last time we'll say this . . . in the wilderness, your physical safety is constantly threatened. In that environment, your safety has to be your number-one priority at all times or you will die. So through generations of genetics, parental training, and extensive cultural reinforcement, your brain has developed a craving for safety that cannot be ignored.

The Connection between Geography and Mentality

If you really were a hunter/gatherer, this default setting would manifest *geographically*. You and your clan would inhabit a very small patch of ground called your home territory. A home territory is surprisingly small – maybe 10–20 square miles, like the size of a typical small town. And over the course of your life, you and your clan would never ever leave that home territory unless you were forced to. That small patch of ground would exert an incredibly strong pull on you. This makes sense, because in your home territory you have advantages, right? You know all the good hiding places, you know where all the good berries grow, and so forth. For survival purposes, the craving for safety is brilliantly effective.

But nowadays this safety wiring manifests *psychologically*, and it works against you. Specifically, this is the wiring that creates your *comfort zone*. Now it's not wrong to have a comfort zone – everyone has them ingrained in their brains.

The trouble here is that you're looking for growth . . . and *no growth happens inside your comfort zone.*

Growth versus Comfort: A Losing Battle?

Think about it: Every single thing that creates progress for you is either uncomfortable, risky, or both. Examples:

- You want to grow your book of business? You'll have to do some prospecting, which is uncomfortable and emotionally risky.
- Want to make your body stronger? You'll have to tax your muscles in ways that hurt.
- Want to grow your net worth or save money for the future? You'll have to sacrifice some creature comforts now, which feels risky to your brain.

Moving forward will regularly require you to choose between something that creates progress but is risky/uncomfortable, versus something that is easy/safe/comfortable but leaves you stuck. And by default, your brain will want to choose easy/

safe/comfortable 100 percent of the time . . . not 90 percent but *100 hundred percent of the time.* This is why people so often end up stuck, stagnant, and feeling unable to break out.

Stuck Is the Byproduct of Safe

Nobody ever chooses "Stuck" consciously – you've never woken up on January 1 and made a New Year's resolution in which you said "I really want this new year to suck exactly as much as last year." But what we constantly do is unconsciously choose the thoughts and habits that feel comfortable, familiar, and thereby safe . . . and feeling stuck is the byproduct, every single time.

Summary

Your brain has three major default settings:

1. The tendency to overemphasize negative inputs
2. The tendency to be easily consumed with urgent events
3. The constant craving for safety over progress

These will get in the way of your progress. Be honest: Can you recognize these default settings showing up in your life? We hope you can, because recognition and awareness are always the first step to making an upgrade. You can't escape from a prison that you don't know you're in, right?

Some Bad News, Some Good News, and Some Really Good News

The bad news here is that you have these default settings, and they will run the show if you let them. Sorry to be a bummer, but it's true.

The good news here – and please hear this clearly – is that you are 100 percent *not* a victim of your default settings. You're not a machine that is compelled to run on its programming. Above all, you are a human being. And as human beings, all of us have been given the abilities to make choices, take actions, and learn from our experiences.

And if you can do those things – choose, act, and learn – it means that you have the capacity to take the programs you've been given and *rewrite them yourself*, so that they can bear whatever fruit you want them to.

The really good news here is that by rewriting these programs in small ways, you can affect massive improvements and upgrades. And that's what you're going to learn next.

Chapter Review

- Your brain has "default settings," just like a computer. Some of them serve as excellent survival mechanisms, but are horribly counterproductive in your quest for greatness.
- Your brain tends to overemphasize negative and underemphasize positive inputs.
- Your brain is easily consumed by urgent events, at the expense of the important one.
- Your brain craves safety over progress.

5

The 2-Millimeter Principle and the Recipe for a Breakthrough

It's our hope that in this part of *Master Your Mind*, you've gained some foundational understanding of why you operate the way you do, along with some of the internal roadblocks you face. We're about to transition out of foundational understanding and into specific methods and principles, many of which you can implement immediately. Let's end this first part of *Master Your Mind* with two concepts that will make you more likely to take action. In this chapter we introduce the 2-millimeter principle, and then the recipe for a breakthrough.

The 2-Millimeter Principle

> The inches we need are *everywhere* around us. They are in every break of the game, every minute, every second.
>
> —*Al Pacino, Any Given Sunday*

The 2-millimeter (2 mm) principle, originally taught to me (Roger) as the "Winning Edge Theory," sets forth the idea that *tiny changes, in the right places, can cause a gigantic difference in the end result.* I started calling it the 2-millimeter principle when I realized something about golf.

Think about a golf ball, sitting motionless on the tee. Now consider the driver, arcing down to send that ball down the fairway, and you'll begin to understand how little differences can make a big difference, and also why golf drives people crazy. If the driver strikes the ball dead center *and* at a perfect 90-degree angle, you get a straight shot directly down the center of the fairway. If you make that shot, you'll get a feeling of tremendous satisfaction and, depending on whom you're golfing with, possibly win some wagers.

Now alter that picture just slightly: imagine that, instead of a 90-degree angle, the club face strikes the ball at an 85-degree angle (that's less than a 5 percent shift) that ball will be not just a little off the fairway, but w-a-a-ay off. You might not even find the ball, you'll definitely be out of position, and you'll feel, well, not tremendously satisfied. One of our clients (who's an avid golfer) described that tiny shift of less than 5 percent as "the difference between elation and frustration." If we're talking about a professional golfer, that tiny shift can literally mean the difference between first place and 10th place . . . and hundreds of thousands of dollars in prize money.

Another example: During the writing of this book, the Kentucky Derby (and then later the Triple Crown) was won by a horse named Justify. The purse in the Derby was $2,000,000, and the winning horse got 62 percent. The remaining 38 percent was split up between the next four horses, and anyone placing out of the top five won zero dollars. Here are the results from that race.

Kentucky Derby Results List

- **Win ($1.24 million):** Justify (2:04.20); Jockey: Mike Smith; Trainer: Bob Baffert
- **Place ($400,000):** Good Magic (–2½ lengths); Jockey: Jose Ortiz; Trainer: Chad Brown

- **Show ($200,000):** Audible (–2½ lengths); Jockey: Javier Castellano; Trainer: Todd Pletcher
- **4th ($100,000):** Instilled Regard (–4¼ lengths); Jockey: Drayden Van Dyke; Trainer: Jerry Hollendorfer
- **5th ($60,000):** My Boy Jack (–7 lengths); Jockey: Kent Desormeaux; Trainer: J. Keith Desormeaux
- **6th:** Bravazo (–8 lengths); Jockey: Luis Contreras; Trainer: D. Wayne Lukas

The 2 mm principle is in full effect on this list, in several ways. First, note the huge difference in prize money between Justify and Good Magic . . . that's an $804,000 difference! Then understand that the margin of victory (2½ lengths, which in horse racing is a pretty decisive victory) is a matter of less than two seconds, and you can see where a small difference caused a huge difference in the end result – a less than 2 percent edge in time created a 300 percent difference in prize money.

For a less glamorous but even more striking look, check out the difference between fifth and sixth. My Boy Jack finished one length in front of Bravazo, and that's a time difference of under one second. My Boy Jack took home $60,000. Bravazo? Nada. So in this event, a less than 1 percent edge in time caused an *infinity* percent difference in prize money.

And that's what life is like, too. As a reader of ours, it's likely that you operate in a highly competitive environment, one where your "margins of victory" can be slim . . . and create orders of magnitude differences, sometimes *infinity percent* differences. You give a slightly better presentation than "the other guy," or follow up with a client just slightly bette. . . and you get *all* the business as opposed to none. You make that *one* extra call every day, and it adds up to thousands, maybe tens of thousands of extra dollars in your pocket at the end of the year. You do *a couple* of things to rewire your brain for more focus/energy/creativity, and six months later your life looks totally different.

And please consider this: We're not just waxing poetic or talking about theories . . . these are actual results that we see our clients achieve.

Al Pacino, in the football movie *Any Given Sunday*, gives an iconic locker-room speech (it's worth watching the movie just for this scene, as long as you don't mind a little cussing.)

> The inches we need are *everywhere* around us. They are in every break of the game, every minute, every second. On this team, we fight for that inch. On this team, we tear ourselves, and everyone around us, to pieces for that inch. We *claw* with our fingernails for that inch. 'Cause we know, when we add up all those inches, that's going to make the f—g difference between *winning* and *losing*, between *living* and *dying*.

It's the 2 mm principle, and we hope you find it inspiring. You don't need to do everything differently in order to get radically different results. You need to do a few things different, but not everything. As you're reading the rest of *Master Your Mind*, be looking for where your 2 mm, or your "inches," are, and upgrade them just a little. Small shifts there will make a huge difference.

And if you're wondering where to start looking, we'll recommend you begin with improving your recipe for a breakthrough.

The Recipe for a Breakthrough

Fundamentally, if you are reading this book, it's a good indication that you are looking to create a mental breakthrough. Not just an epiphany, but a breakthrough, that will show up in your results. You have gotten yourself to a certain point, and the next stage of the game is beyond what you are capable of either thinking about or achieving on your own.

In our work over the years, we've identified that when it comes to achieving a mental (and therefore results) breakthrough, there are three key components that are required. These are to:

- Get help.
- Get invested.
- Get away.

Let's take a look at each of these components individually, and then show you a perfect example of all of them at work.

Get Help

This is not a new concept, but the very first thing that is needed in order to create a breakthrough is to *get help*. Specifically, help can be found in the form of a coach or an accountability partner, someone who can look at your situation through a different, outside, and hopefully unbiased set of eyes and help guide you down the best path to success. Someone who isn't afraid to hold your feet to the fire, and someone you trust to do that for you. For extra credit, get your help from someone who has been where you are and has gotten to where you want to go.

The reason this is step #1 is because you simply aren't capable of getting where you want to go on your own. For so many reasons, our brains and our behaviors are controlled by our beliefs. These beliefs come from your experiences and your reactions to them.

Right, wrong, or indifferent, these experiences and beliefs create patterns. It's when we get comfortable and familiar with a pattern that stagnation kicks in. One of our favorite lines to use with clients is "I'm not telling you anything you don't already know . . . ," but we've lost track of the number of times their reply has been, "I know, I just needed to hear it again from someone else in order for it to kick in." There is no shame in getting outside help. There is nothing to be afraid of or embarrassed about.

While sitting in to observe my (Robb's) first oral surgery, I was told by the surgeon, "Okay, Robb, when you start to feel like you are going to pass out, just let us know. We're *really* good at catching people! And don't worry, everyone does it, so don't try and be a hero." At first I responded, "Whatever, I'll be fine!" but 36 minutes later, I can tell you I was *all* about letting them know I needed a little help to stay conscious. If I had not slowed down my thinking and behavior to be available for help, I likely would have been a *major* distraction to the surgeon and his team while they were trying to complete the procedure. The good news is I did *not* pass out (It was definitely touch-and-go for a few minutes), the team was able to finish the procedure with no interruptions, and the doctor and his team and I now have a really fun story to laugh about and bond over!

Get Invested

In order to achieve a breakthrough, you will be making a moderately uncomfortable investment in yourself. We use the term "invest" purposefully here. Most people, when they hear the term "invest" automatically think, "Well, how much money is this going to cost me?" Unfortunately, that's only half of the equation (or less). The bigger and sometimes more uncomfortable investment you need to make in yourself is related to time.

Over the course of your life you will make money and lose money, earn it and spend it. You can always replenish whatever finances you acquire and burn through. You can't do the same with time. Once it is gone, it is gone. My favorite analogy compares a lifetime to a roll of toilet paper. Once the roll starts getting smaller, it gets used up more and more quickly. Once it is used up, it is *gone*, and you *definitely* don't want to try and re-use it.

Our time is the single most valuable asset we have (and it can be argued if we even "have" it at all). The whole premise of this book is tied to the idea that in order to achieve faster results, we need to slow down. The same thing goes when investing your time. So many people we know get caught up in their day-to-day activities that the idea of proactively carving out a specific amount of time to invest in themselves seems like a waste of time. Unfortunately, this simply isn't true. Don't believe me? Read the chapter on the two-hour solution and tell me that it didn't work for Aubrey, or for anyone flying on an airplane, for that matter.

Making an uncomfortable investment might present you with a number or timeframe that at first glance kind of freaks you out. You aren't really sure how you are going to budget/afford/come up with that amount. And your first verbal or mental response could be "But I don't want to do that."

However, once you spend 30–60 seconds actually thinking about the return on investment, your brain says, "Wait . . . that's not that bad! I think I can figure this out!" For a lot of our clients, the thought of setting aside two hours every week is ludicrous. But then, once they understand what that two hours will do for them, it becomes *really* easy for them to start finding little pockets of time that, when added up, typically equal about five to six hours. Sometimes that's in just one day!

Financially, where can you "rob Peter to pay Paul"? Can you give up your fancy Italian-sounding-but-not-at-all-Italian coffee drink? How about one less restaurant meal per month? Or one less drink at the bar? If the achievement of a mental breakthrough is worth it to you, what can you squeeze out of your life in order to make it happen? Is the juice worth the squeeze? In almost every case we've come across, the answer has been a resounding *yes*.

Get Away

Possibly the easiest of all the components to understand and justify, "get away," has a couple of different definitions. And they are all the right definition.

If you read the introduction to *Train Your Brain for Success*, you are familiar with the infographic (shown in Figure 5.1) about comfort zones and where magic happens.

Figure 5.1 The Magic Happens Outside of Your Comfort Zone

While not inherently bad, your comfort zone is often the only thing that limits – or more accurately, prohibits – you from creating a mental breakthrough on your own. Your comfort zone is based on familiarity. Every decision you make gets made on an unconscious level based on your familiarity with a certain experience or food or temperature or amount of resistance or fun or misery.

So the easiest way to distance yourself from that familiarity is to get away. What do I mean?

- Get away from your office.
- Get away from your colleagues.
- Get away from your family.
- Get away from your routine.
- Get away from your time zone.
- Get away from your diet.
- Get away from your TV.
- Get away from whatever "story" you are currently believing.

Call it an opportunity for a new perspective, or a new outlook, whatever works for you. But in order for you to "scramble your brain" so you are mentally available for a breakthrough, you need to get away from whatever you do, or from wherever you normally do it. Ever notice that the majority of personal development retreats typically take place at secluded locations or at a luxury resort or island? It's not a coincidence. The types of curriculum that are shared at these require participants to be in an open state of mind in order to try instituting the changes that they learn about. Some of the best conferences I have been asked to speak at were held in places that offered a ton of entertainment: Las Vegas, Hawaii, the Wisconsin Dells, Pigeon Forge, Miami, New Orleans, Walt Disney World. Conference planners know that in order for their attendees to "get the most out of the experience," there has to be a lot more to the experience. Incidentally, this whole idea ties in to what we advise, about taking time off for renewal.

Its Not All Resorts and All-Inclusives

But many of you reading this book either won't or don't have the opportunity to attend a conference at an expensive resort or destination. Not a problem. Here are a few real life (and alternative) examples of what "getting away" might look like:

For a lot of our coaching clients, getting away means setting up our calls at a coffee shop or at home instead of at the office, where they might be distracted.

- A sales professional decides to go commando in an effort to break a string of no-result presentations.
- Baseball's "Rally Cap."
- The Beatles going to India for new inspiration.
- Holding a meeting at a coworking space or restaurant instead of the office.
- *Not* turning on the news in the first 10 minutes that you are awake.

Case Study: The Perfect Getaway

From Robb:

Probably the best representation of the results you can expect from "getting away" comes from one of my favorite organizations, the Seattle Study Club. Founded in 1993 by Dr Michael Cohen, the Seattle Study Club is a membership-based organization that brings together the greatest clinical, practice management, and personal development minds in Comprehensive Dentistry. There are over 250 chapters/clubs all over the world and it is one of the most recognized and respected organizations in dentistry. Its mission is to cultivate excellence in comprehensive dentistry. Every speaker, every partner, every piece of content that is shared is thoroughly vetted before being introduced to members. When I was first introduced to the Seattle Study Club, I was told by one of its founding members, "You know it takes about 10 years to become a speaker for this group. And that's after you get referred in." I made it in three.

If you are still struggling to understand the group, imagine that a country club and a mastermind group had a love child, and *only* the clinically best and brightest dentists in the world were allowed to join. That's Seattle Study Club distilled down. I have had the honor and privilege to travel all over the country speaking for its members, and I am blessed to call many of them my friends.

In addition to the monthly meetings that are held in each club, Seattle Study Club hosts its annual Symposium, open to all its members. To quote the late Keith Jackson, this event is "The granddaddy of them al-l-l-l!"

This week-long event features a lineup of unparalleled clinical, practice management, and professional development presentations. The event is always held at a premier luxury property: Ritz Carlton, Four Seasons, Fairmont, and Waldorf Astoria have all hosted the Symposium. I met a sales executive for a luxury hotel brand at a conference where I was a speaker a few years ago, and she shared with me that there is always a *major* competition among all the brands to try and land the contract for the Symposium. As you can tell, this event is a huge deal.

The reason it is a huge deal is that the attendees *know* that they are going to walk away with a *ton* of information, insights, and new relationships that will help them continue to grow their individual practices.

Let's break down the Seattle Study Club's annual Symposium into the three components that contribute to achieving a breakthrough.

Get Help

As I mentioned earlier, the speaker lineup consistently includes some of the top speakers available anywhere in the world. Doctors who attend have the opportunity to learn new ideas, new techniques, and new approaches from these sessions. There is a *massive* networking and mastermind element to the symposium as the experienced doctors are always available to lend advice to newer or up-and-coming dentists.

At the last Symposium I attended, I overheard one of my doctor friends chatting with one of the presenters (a world-renowned oral surgeon). I didn't catch all of the conversation, but the part I did hear was, "Doctor, I just wanted to come over and meet you personally and thank you. I saw your presentation five years ago on the ___ procedure, and I have to tell you that your presentation singlehandedly changed how I approach that procedure and the success rate that my practice has experienced as a result of switching to it."

Pretty powerful stuff, in a scenario that never would have happened had my friend not been in attendance (at both events)!

Get Invested

The Symposium is not cheap. Registration is $4,000 per person. That's just registration for the curriculum. That does not include travel or lodging or all the meals. And did I mention that it's always held at a luxury property? In talking with the doctors who regularly attend, I've learned that it's not uncommon to have a five-figure folio at the end of the trip. Yes, these folks are well compensated for their work, but $10K is still $10K. In the words of my friend Bob (Chapter 12 Bob), "You know, it's not the $4,000 registration or even the $600-per-night rooms, it's all these damn $1,500 dinners we end up having! But I tell you what, the time I get to spend with my friends and the case studies we get to share makes it all worth it!"

But even if there is a $10,000 or even $20,000 final bill, that's not even remotely close to the total investment that goes into attending. All these doctors run practices. And the success of those practices is based on their ability to be in the operating room providing treatment (i.e., surgeries, extractions, placing implants, etc.). One of my friends owns a multi-office practice. It's been reported that his is the #1 revenue-producing practice in the country, with his business regularly recording $100,000 of revenue in a single *day*. And these are elective procedures – there is no insurance to cover these costs. For comparison, that would be like a Realtor selling five million-dollar homes in a day.

Or a life insurance agent writing twenty million-dollar policies in a day. Or a car dealership selling 200 new cars in a day.

So when you factor in his time out of the practice and the potential lost revenue, the cost of attending, the cost of his team attending, and all the little things like plane tickets and hotel rooms and meals and sightseeing and whatever services he might sign up for or orders he might place with vendors, that might roll up to almost a million dollars for a week at Symposium. But when I asked him why he would spend so much, he didn't even pause to think about it. He looked me right in the eye and said, "I'm not spending anything, I'm investing in myself and my team and my business and I know that if we learn one new thing and put it to use in our practice, it's going to pay for itself. I know because I've been coming to this event every year for 15 years, and every year it is worth it!"

Get Away

If you have read the other two areas where Symposium fits the mold for creating a breakthrough, this part is a no-brainer. I won't bore you with repeating the same details over and over. But I will share this point. Having become friends with the executive team of Seattle Study Club group, I have learned there is a reason why they host events at the properties that they choose.

In an effort to keep their members enrolled year after year, the team knows that it's the *experience* of being at Symposium that makes it so magical. They know their members are looking to create memories and stories and traditions that simply cannot happen in their normal day-to-day locations. By hosting the event at a premier destination, with premier talent and speakers, the Seattle Study Club group allows its members to get into a relaxed, open-minded state in order to get the most out of their investment. And to be clear, a lot of the entertainment is set up to get their minds *off* the clinical approach to their business. World-class entertainers like Tommy Emmanuel, Jake Shimabukuro, and others are making appearances at the event. There is a professional emcee running the show. Competitions, game shows, and social events round out the agenda. And *that* is the reason folks have been attending for over 25 years.

For some of you reading this, the idea of Symposium is so far outside your norm that it is hard to fathom taking all that time away from work, including all the effort and expense of getting there. If that sounds like you, it's time to find your own "Symposium" and create the mental breakthrough you are seeking. Maybe it's a seven-day fishing trip off the coast of Southern California. Maybe it's participating in the 24-hour Moab mountain bike race or the L'etape du Tour or your first half or full marathon. Maybe it's attending the NAIFA National Convention or the NAR Annual Conference or whatever your industry's biggest event is. Whatever it is, it's not sitting right in front of you, in your office, or even in your hometown. You have to go out and find it. But once you do, I can guarantee you will thank yourself. And so will the people around you.

For more information on Seattle Study Club, visit www.seattlestudyclub.com.

Chapter Review

- In order to achieve a mental, and therefore results-oriented breakthrough, focus on the following "gets":
- Get help.
- Get invested.
- Get away.

PART II

Slow Down the Game: Counterintuitive Strategies and Tactics That Really Work

The rest of Master *Your Mind* is devoted to tactics you can put to work immediately. You'll see that many of them involve variations on the principle of slowing down to speed up, and all of them are counterintuitive. "Counterintuitive" basically means that on the surface they can seem backward.

"Slow down to speed up" sounds, well – backward. Likely, so do these ideas:

- Saying *no* gets more *yesses.*
- Working *less* allows you to achieve *more.*
- Stealing two hours for yourself allows you to give 10 hours (or more) to everyone who's important to you.
- Shutting your mouth entirely makes for the best "presentation."
- Having a *less* detailed plan makes your plan *better.*
- *Huge* results often start out microscopically *small.*
- *Pen and paper* are actually infinitely smarter than a *computer* and the *Internet.*

If these concepts sound backward to you, no problem. We're imagining that you don't really care about being "normal," and you're much more interested in getting great results.

Note: *Zero* percent of what you're about to learn is theoretical – it's all been proven to work. The following six chapters lay out practices that we actually use ourselves, that our clients all over the world use, and that top performers in multiple industries use . . . *and they work.*

So, let's go!

6

Master Your Mind by Mastering Your Input: Programming Your Mind for Automatic Results

Garbage in, garbage out.

—*Anonymous*

Take care of the beginning and the end, and the middle will take care of itself.

—*Dan Moore, president of Southwestern Advantage*

You've heard the saying "Garbage in, garbage out" (GIGO). It seems that it originated as a slang phrase among math and computer science experts, but it's been used to describe the relationship between input and output in a myriad situations.

Wikipedia offers the definition:

> In computer science, garbage in, garbage out (GIGO) is where flawed or nonsense input data produces nonsense output or "garbage."
>
> The principle also applies more generally to all analysis and logic, in that arguments are unsound if their premises are flawed.

Techtarget.com describes it this way:

> GIGO (garbage in, garbage out) is a concept common to computer science and mathematics: the quality of output is determined by the quality of the input. So, for example, if a mathematical equation is improperly stated, the answer is unlikely to be correct. Similarly, if incorrect data is input to a program, the output is unlikely to be informative.

And the concept really applies when it comes to *you*. In your life, the quality of your output is a direct result of the quality of your input. Consider your physical well-being. If you eat too much fast food food, you will end up undernourished, weak, and probably overweight and ill.

And the principle shows up in the exact same way in your mind . . . what you input into your brain will determine what you get out of your results. We devote this chapter to helping you upgrade all your input sources, and specifically alter your routines at the most critical times for proper input.

Your Major Mental Input Sources

We've long taught that one of your most effective Mindset Management tools is your ability to manage *mental input*. You've got two general categories of input sources: Your *internal* input sources essentially originate from you, whereas your *external* sources come from your environment.

Internal Input

You have three major input sources that come from within you, and that you have the highest levels of influence over: your thoughts, your language (a.k.a. your self-talk), and your physical actions. These three interact with each other instantaneously and continuously. One of our great mentors, Ed Foreman, says that "you can not have the inkling of a notion of a thought without every cell in your body responding. Your body and your emotions are eavesdropping on all your thoughts."

We've been taught that:

- Thoughts dictate emotions (or feelings).
- Emotions create actions.
- Actions create results.

Thoughts===>Emotions===>Actions===>Results

. . . which is pretty accurate, but we're learning that the reality is more three-dimensional, with feedback loops everywhere. It actually looks more like this:

- *Thoughts* dictate *emotions.*
- *Emotions* create *self-talk* (and more thoughts).
- *Self-talk* creates *actions* (and more thoughts and more emotions).
- *Actions* directly create *results* (and more thoughts, more emotions, and different self-talk).

Critical Point

You have only two options with the effects of these input sources. You can either **intentionally** make them **uplifting, positive, and helpful,** or you are **unintentionally** allowing them to be **self-defeating, negative, and even destructive**. There is no middle ground. This means that your inputs are either helping or hurting; never are they neutral.

Control the Controllables

So for the purpose of programming your internal inputs, consider which of these you have the most direct *control* over. If you can control what's most controllable, the others will tend to fall in line by themselves.

So, do you control your thoughts? We'd suggest these are among the *least* controllable of your input sources, at least if you approach them directly. Think about it . . . the whole premise of this book is your "Runaway Brain," which by definition means your thoughts have a life of their own! Your thoughts are difficult to control directly.

How about your results? Again, we'll propose that results like money, sales, the cleanliness of your house, and how much you can bench press are (unfortunately) not under your direct control. Results are a *byproduct* of your actions, so you *influence* them, but there are other factors that can impact them.

The internal inputs you control most directly are your words (your self-talk) and your physical actions. Fundamentally, this is where we focus our efforts with our coaching clients. We help them craft specific actions – some daily, some weekly, some quarterly – and then words to say or read, and then develop consistency and accountability around these. When you influence your words and your actions, the feedback loops take over. What happens then is that you create a virtuous cycle where your thoughts, feelings, actions, self-talk, *and* your results all improve together.

Improving your self-talk is such a big deal that it's the subject of the next chapter, so we'll leave it alone here. Let's focus on physical actions that we know will raise your energy and literally change your vibrational frequency for the better. This is not an all-inclusive list, but here are some things you can *do*, all of which will boost your mood and help rewire your brain predictably *and* can be done pretty much anywhere, without being obnoxious or making you feel weird:

- Breathe deeply
- Smile
- Laugh
- Walk
- Perform light physical exercise like pushups, situps, or yoga
- Stand like a superhero
- Bounce
- Drink a big glass of water
- Stretch
- Read affirmations
- Read anything uplifting/inspiring/educational
- Writing: goals, gratitude list, or journaling
- Give a sincere compliment to someone
- Any random act of kindness

There are infinite variations on how you do each of these – customizing a full-on "programming ritual" with our clients is a pillar of our coaching. For now, just know that:

- These actions can be done, alone or in combination, *anytime* for a little positive programming that's guaranteed to work.
- There's never a bad time, but there is a best time for these which is why at least some of them will be part of "Winning the Beginning" of your day (coming up soon).

Let's look next at influences that come from outside you.

External Input

Your major external input sources consist of:

- What you read
- What you watch
- What you listen to
- Who you hang around with – what they say to you/about you, and how they make you feel

Critical Point

You only have two options in receiving these input sources. You can either intentionally make them uplifting, positive, and helpful, or you can unintentionally allow them to be self-defeating, negative and even destructive. There is no middle ground. It means that your inputs are either helping or hurting; never are they neutral.

That may have sounded a little repetitive . . . let that be a clue. It's especially tricky to get the external inputs right because so many entities are competing to influence your mind, and most of them don't really have your best interest at heart.

Competition for Your Mind Is Fiercer Than Ever Before

More and more in this hyperconnected world, you have to operate while bombarded by a myriad input sources:

1. Advertising from companies who want your money
2. Media sources who just want you to pay attention to their channel . . . so that you are exposed to #1
3. Agencies, bureaucracy, and regulations
4. Lots of people who have their own agendas
5. Lots and lots and lots of people who just want to whine and complain so you feel bad for them

I'm not saying that all of these entities are "out to get you," but some of them in fact are. And *all* of them are actively working to direct your focus and program your thoughts, feelings, and actions.

It used to be much easier to avoid some of these unhelpful external input sources, but today it's nearly impossible. So it's vital that you take responsibility and choose some external inputs that serve you. Again, you will need to be intentional about this: *Inputs that serve you cannot break through the clutter unless you're purposeful, consistent, and downright aggressive in helping them break through.* You must not only invite helpful inputs into your mind, sometimes you have to drag them in through a crowd.

Here are some proven and simple ways you can achieve this, utilizing your natural alpha and theta times at the beginning of your day, at the end of your day, and even throughout your day.

- Listen to music that inspires or moves you.
- Listen to a podcast or audio in your car.
- Read a book (what a concept!).
- Avoid "the news" like the plague.

Winning the Beginning of Your Day

Champions are made when nobody is watching.

—*John Wooden, 10-time NCAA championship basketball coach*

Your first critical window for programming your mind happens in the quiet part of the morning, when it's just you and the new day. This window opens the moment your eyes open to begin the morning.

"The First Hour of the Day Is *Mine*"

Chris Sullivan, cofounder of Outback Steakhouse, is an amazing person and an unbelievably successful entrepreneur. Even a quick Internet search reveals a great number of accomplishments: He started a handful of well-known restaurant chains, contributed and participated in charity/community work, and now oversees organizations with thousands of employees. By all accounts he's a wonderful guy, very balanced, very grounded, and very much at peace with himself. He makes success look easy.

When asked at a breakfast event "What's your secret?" his reply was enlightening.

> Most of the hours of my day belong to other people- I'm answering questions, helping leaders make decisions, working with my team, attending meetings, et cetera. Plus there's family, which is super important for me to spend time with. So *a lot* of my hours belong to other people. The only way I can make sure that's sustainable? *The first hour of the day... that one is mine.*

Sage advice, and you'll hear similar sentiments from nearly every significant leader, thinker, or top producer. They may describe it in different words, but those whom we want to emulate have specific routines that help them to *win* the beginning of their day. Here's why that's so smart.

Remember Alpha and Theta?

Think back to our discussion of brain wave patterns, and how your "subconscious elephant" makes results happen. Remember the different states:

> High alpha . . . you remember everything whether you want to or not.
>
> High theta . . . inputs go directly to your subconscious whether you want them to or not.

Recall that your first high theta/alpha period happens in the first 30 minutes of your day. Now you can see why so much importance is placed on starting your day the right way. Your first 30–60 minutes of each day set the tone for your brain and your results for the whole rest of the day.

And here's the deal – you know it's coming. The first hour of the day happens *every single day*, right? It might help you or it might hurt you, but it's going to do *something* to you every morning, and you get to choose. So don't miss this golden opportunity to rewire your brain in a big way. If you'd like to learn our entire 15-step process for starting the day, the time that we call the Power Hour, check out Chapter 17 of *Train Your Brain for Success.*

Fundamentally, the key here is to be systematic, consistent, and aggressively protective of what you allow into your mind during this period. Here's how:

You Snooze, You Lose

Let's start with the very beginning of the beginning of the morning . . . *ditch the snooze alarm, and just get up.* I know we're running the risk of irritating you (people tend to get worked up when we tell them to knock it off with the snooze button), but come on. . . . The extra nine minutes of "sleep" you're giving yourself are simply not helping you. Number one, you're not actually sleeping, and number two what you're really doing during that nine minutes is likely the worst possible thing you can do in that borderline theta brain wave time.

You're fretting, worrying, and resisting the day, when your subconscious is listening most closely. With your actions and your words, you're essentially lying there saturating your subconscious with thoughts like:

- "I'm so-o-o tired."
- "I don't want to get up."
- "Work sucks."

And so on. At that time, your subconscious just slurps up all that negativity and self-pity, in such a way that *those thoughts dominate your entire day.*

So knock it off. Act like a grown person and *get up*. You don't need to *leap* out of bed with a smile on your face and a song in your heart (though it's worth trying), but if you and your subconscious elephant are lying in bed stewing, fretting, and resisting, then stumbling toward your toothbrush is much better.

How about trying a small exercise beginning tomorrow morning. It's a very small step, and nobody even needs to know you did it. Tomorrow morning, when the alarm goes off, just gently put your feet on the floor and say to yourself the words that we say to ourselves every single day: "*It's gonna be a great day.*"

You can mumble this, slur it, enunciate it, or shout it—it doesn't matter. Starting your day with the little six-word sentence

"*It's gonna be a great day*" does so much to rewire your brain for a successful day that it's not even funny. The entire next chapter is about how to make the voices in your head into your allies, but in case you skip that chapter, just try this one little phrase when you get up in the morning, and tell us if it doesn't make a difference. We promise it will – just get up.

A Positive Use for the Snooze Button

In case you can't tell, in general we're not big fans of the snooze button. There is, however, one use of it that we found that's *so* good we have to include it. Darren Hardy, in his outstanding book *The Compound Effect*, describes how he hits the snooze button *every single day*! What he does for the nine minutes between alarms is genius: He lies in bed and thinks of things he's grateful for. He's not making lists in his mind, not stressing over the events of yesterday, or worrying about what might happen today or thinking about anything other than what he is thankful for. This method would actually give your subconscious the best fuel it can have to run on all day

If you can pull this off consistently, we'd highly encourage you to use the snooze alarm in just this manner. If you can't direct your thoughts to gratitude, though, just get up.

Stay Unplugged as Long as Possible

Once you're up, you'll want to make sure that the first 30- to 60-minute window of the day is insulated and protected from stress, worry, and negativity as much as possible. The simplest way to effect this is to stay unplugged as long as you can.

Just stay away from screens for the first hour of the day: It will change your life. Think about what comes from your screens . . .

- Email
- "Reply All"
- Office politics
- Gossip
- Mindless chatter

- The "news"
- Your friends' raging political opinions
- People asking for "suggestions" that are really just poorly concealed pleas for sympathy

Yes, we're aware that there are amazing and inspiring things that can be found on the Interwebbz – we'll get there in a minute – but what comes from your screens *by default* is overwhelmingly stressful/negative. We're aware that checking email 30 seconds after waking is easy to disguise as "getting a jump on the day." But seriously . . . do you really need to be "checking in" at 5:30 a.m.? More important, do you want to even risk that much stress and negativity pouring into your mind when your mind is at its very most receptive? Is it really worth it?

So come on – for the first half hour of your day, leave the TV off. Don't check email. Don't get on social media. Definitely don't watch the news. Treat the quiet part of the morning like it's meant to be treated – with care and love and gratitude. Do this and it'll treat you the same way . . . all day long.

"Well, If I Can't Use My Screens . . . What Am I Supposed to Do?"

First, this is the lament of teenagers. So unless you actually are 14 years old, just stop. Please.

Second, we're so glad you asked. There are actually a ton of things you can use to replace "screen time" for the first part of your day, which have been well researched and utilized in combination by the most successful people on earth.

To be clear: A morning ritual involving some combination of these elements is the single biggest common denominator among the most successful people in the world. Ask any successful entrepreneur, leader, top producer, professional athlete, or otherwise wildly effective human about their "morning routine." They may all have different answers, but they will have an answer. If you currently have no systematic intentional way of getting up in the morning, this is exactly where you need to start mastering your mind.

What should your routine consist of? To a certain degree it depends on who you ask. If you read Hal Elrod's fantastic book *The Miracle Morning*, you'll learn about his six-step S.A.V.E.R.S model. Tim Ferriss, in his enormous monolith of content, often talks about three (or four or five, depending on which blog post you're reading) things he does to win the morning. If you read our book *Train Your Brain for Success*, you'll learn about the Power Hour, which consists of 15 small victories that start your day "undefeated" and feeling unstoppable.

There's a *ton* of advice out there that we've drawn from over the years to develop our own rituals. For now, we recommend adopting some combination of the following activities to fill up your theta and alpha windows:

1. Affirmations: verbal, written, recorded, or all of these (covered in-depth in the next chapter).
2. Gratitude: taking a moment to truly appreciate the promise of a new day can sometimes be all you need.
3. Exercise: stretching, yoga, calisthenics, running, or whatever gets you moving and feels good.
4. Drink a big glass of water.
5. Make a really nice pot of coffee or tea.
6. Read and/or listen to something uplifting, inspiring, or enriching.
7. Read and/or listen to something that makes you laugh.
8. Writing/journaling.
9. The Daily Big Six (see Chapter 9 on The Two-Hour Solution, and Chapter 12 of *Train Your Brain for Success*)
10. Meditation: There are a myriad possibilities for how to meditate.
11. Visualization: Focus on your goals and how you'd like your day to go.
12. Make your bed or otherwise do something to assert control over chaos and disorganization.

Of course this isn't a totally comprehensive list, there are lots of possibilities. Is it necessary to do *all* of these? Of course not, though it's not impossible and might be worth a shot. For starters, pick two to five of the above that you're not doing currently and fold them into the first 30–60 minutes of your morning.

Here's our secret sauce for these morning rituals: As you do any of these activities, stop for a moment and really notice that you did them. Pat yourself on the back and celebrate each step as a small, private victory. This might seem silly, but trust us, it's potent. When it comes to boosting your self-confidence, your energy, and your overall attractiveness, there's almost nothing that beats catching yourself doing something right. Noticing even one small victory makes you see yourself as stronger and more in control. String together a handful of actions that you notice as wins, and you generate authentic momentum that compounds throughout the rest of your day. String together a few days like that and you've got a really successful week. String together a handful of weeks like that and you've physically rewired a new level of effectiveness and vibrancy into your life . . . and it's become a habit.

Small steps to start your day really add up to something special. Capitalize on that opportunity.

Like we said, there's a ton that's been written recently about starting your day correctly. The other huge opportunity for programming is not discussed as often, and it's not nearly as well known. If you become mindful of the *end* of your day, you've got a solid opportunity to further distance yourself from the norm. Let's explore . . .

Winning the End of Your Day

If you want to be average, learn what the majority does and do that. If you want to be extraordinary, learn what the majority does and *do the opposite*.

—*Unknown genius*

Your other significant alpha/theta window for programming your mind opens when you're transitioning from your waking day into your night of sleep. For the last 30–60 minutes of your day, you've got another excellent chance to wire successful, abundant thoughts into your brain in a way that takes zero time.

As much as the *first* thoughts/actions/words of the day establish the tone for your active day, the *last* thoughts/actions/words of the day establish the tone for your restful night, which is maybe even more important for your subconscious.

See, your subconscious never sleeps – it doesn't need to. So when you're sleeping, your subconscious is incredibly active – it's turning information into long-term memories, it's processing the events of your day, it's working on problems that your conscious mind can't solve by itself, and it's setting you up for success.

It's pretty mind-boggling to think about all the "work" that gets done by your subconscious while you're out cold. When you start programming your subconscious intentionally while heading into your sleep time, your brain will do an amazing number of things to work its magic while you're literally putting forth zero energy. Talk about slowing down to speed up . . . talk about the ultimate ROI on your energy!

To optimize this principle, you've got two main strategies:

1. Transition mindfully and gently.
2. Ask a good question.

Transition Out of Your Day Mindfully and Gently

WARNING!

Here's another place where, if you follow our advice, you will be considered "not normal." The way that we go to bed, the way that our clients go to bed and the way that true top performers go to bed is radically different than the way most people go to bed. If you follow this example you will not be normal . . . but you will thank us profusely after a maximum of one week.

Think about why the morning time is important for programming- You're coming out of delta brain waves, transitioning through theta and alpha to spend most of your day in the hyper-alert, fully stimulated beta state. So in that transitional theta/alpha period, you remember everything or download it directly to your subconscious whether you mean to or not. The same goes for the time where you're winding down for the day, just in reverse order. *The last 30–60 minutes of your day are just as critical as the first 30–60.*

Now consider what usually happens during that time. If you're like most people, you'll go from frantic activity (feeding kids, bringing kids home from practice, working late, commuting, shoving food in your mouth) directly to faceplanting in your pillow, often with booze and TV being the very last inputs you experience for the day. If our clients ever have a hard time waking up full of energy and feeling good, the first place we'll look at is *how they go to bed.* Your morning actually starts the night before, so take care of it.

The "Tech Curfew"

If you want to win the end of your day, for starters, actually decide on a bedtime and stick to it. You give your kids a bedtime because you want them to do well in school the next day, right? Well, give yourself that same advantage!

And then, once you decide when you're hitting the rack, implement a tech curfew. This means that at least 30 minutes before you want to be eyes closed, head on the pillow, the screens are done. Stop staring at computers, TVs, and phones at least a half-hour before you sleep. A full hour is better, but 30 minutes is really helpful.

Lots of research has been done recently on why this is so important, so we won't get into the full dissertation. The basic problem with screen time at night is the *light.* LED screens produce light so bright that it tricks your brain into thinking the sun is still up, so it's not time to be asleep. Screens at night can prevent you from falling asleep, and almost certainly will prevent you from getting good quality rest.

Couple the light issue with the heightened sensitivity of alpha and theta, and the programming that comes from screens at night can be especially counterproductive. Instead, try some of these easy and pleasant activities during this decompression time. Just a few minutes will help you sleep way better and get your subconscious Elephant working for you all night:

- Read a book (what a concept!).
- This is a fantastic time to reread your affirmations.
- Reread your goals.
- Visualize.
- Take a bath or a shower.
- Pillow talk.
- Cuddle.
- Breathe.
- Express gratitude . . .

And then just drift off to sleep, with really good seeds for your subconscious to cultivate all night long.

Three Words That'll Make You *Way* Happier and More Productive

For many professionals, we see that one of the biggest obstacles to mastering their minds is simply that they're poorly rested and therefore exhausted. One of the best things you can do for your productivity is to simply get a good night's sleep. Setting up the correct environment for good sleep is an easy step that you can implement anywhere (especially if you travel), so we thought a short lesson might be valuable.

The creation of a proper sleep environment or "cocoon" is a simple process. It simply involves making sure the room you're sleeping in meets your brain's top three criteria for being able to rest. Those criteria are:

1. **Dark:** Try and remove as much light as possible. Blackout curtains help, as does shutting down TVs, phones, and computers. Even things like alarm clocks and smoke alarm lights can trick your brain, so it's a good idea to cover these up as much as possible.

2. **Quiet:** Your brain is wired to be on high alert for "things that go bump in the night," so the more silence you can bring into your sleeping space, the better for your brain. Some folks find that positive effects can be found with "white noise" like a fan or another monotonous sound, but other than that, try to remove sound of any kind.
3. **Cool:** One of the ways that your body rests is by lowering your body temperature just a bit. Resting in a hot, sweaty environment is nearly impossible, so wherever you can, let your sleeping environment be cool or even cold. Your brain will thank you.

These three simple conditions – dark, quiet, and cool – can truly make a difference in winning the end of your day.

The Question That Sextupled My Productivity Overnight

Here's the secret sauce upgrade for nighttime. It's all about simply asking a good question at the exact right moment, and it takes exactly zero time.

The case study that follows is based on Roger Seip's experience – perhaps you've met him?

If you were to compare Roger's sales effectiveness at the writing of *Master Your Mind* in 2018 to the time when we wrote *Train Your Brain for Success* in 2012, you'd see that he's roughly 600 percent more effective in 2018. This means that every time he has a sales opportunity, on average it produces six times the revenue that it did six years earlier.

Now that might not seem that remarkable, given the long time span. There are two things that make it extremely noteworthy, however:

- As a baseline, in 2012 that metric was already in at least the 95th percentile for his industry.
- The figure didn't improve gradually over time – it actually quantum leaped forward in late 2012/early 2013 and has just stayed there as a permanent upgrade.

How does one bring about such a radical upgrade and then keep it?

From Roger: That upgrade was 100 percent about clarity . . . specifically, clarity about who we were trying to reach. Investing our time in that specific person made all the difference and it literally happened overnight, from one question asked at the right time.

I was at a retreat for authors, receiving incredible coaching and mentoring from Marci Shimoff, the creator of the Chicken Soup for the Woman's Soul series. Marci has sold millions and millions of books, has impacted millions of lives with her speaking, and is a marvelous person to boot, so I was really soaking it all in.

We were on the topic of "Attracting Your Ideal Client," which was something I really needed help with. When I was asked point blank who I was trying to build my business around or sell to, my honest answer was "pretty much anyone who'll write my company a check." It's a terrible answer, but it was pretty true at the time. I was speaking to any group I could get in front of – Realtors, insurance agents, CPAs, teachers, moms, churches, landscapers, investors, renderers (that's the term – I didn't know what they were either, but they could write a check), metal stampers . . . I was all over the map.

So Marci gave us a little exercise to do that night: She encouraged us to ask a question right as we were falling asleep that night. She said it didn't matter whom we were asking the question – God, the Universe, our higher selves, all were fine options. The key was the question itself, and the timing of it.

The question I was prompted to ask was: *Who am I to serve with my business, and how am I to serve them?*

And the key was to ask this question *right as I was falling asleep that night*, and then simply . . . fall asleep. I was encouraged that the answer might be staring me in the face immediately upon waking. If it did appear, then I was supposed to really pay attention, because it's the deepest part of your brain giving you the exact right answer at that moment.

I thought this was a little goofy, but I decided, "What the heck, there's nothing to lose," so I did it. And the result was such a big deal it made my head spin. I did *not* wake up with the answer, but instead it hit me like a bolt of lightning about

30 minutes later while I was running on the treadmill. It was literally like a voice from the deepest part of my brain saying "Yo: You're built to work with:

1. Sales professionals
2. Who are super-serious about growing their book of business . . .
3. But have a good sense of humor, too.

Heeding that answer from my own subconscious has legitimately been worth millions of dollars, and it all came from one question.

You can use the same "question at bedtime" method to answer almost any big question you're wrestling with. "Who's my ideal client?" was a classic example, but there are any number of questions that we've seen our clients ask and then receive answers to that turned out to be exactly right.

- What business to start?
- Should I hire this person or that one?
- What direction should I go?
- Should I buy a building?
- What level of achievement should I be shooting for? How big do I think?

And there are way too many more possibilities to list. Take your question and pose it as you're drifting off to sleep, and don't be surprised if the answer bubbles up soon.

Chapter Review

- Garbage in, garbage out: Managing your mental input sources (both internal and external) is the big key to getting the output you're looking for in your life.
- There are only two options for receiving major input sources . . . either *intentionally* helpful, or *accidentally* negative.
- Program your mind during your highest alpha and theta times of day – that's where you will get the most bang for your buck
- Win the beginning of the day (with a solid morning routine), and you win the whole day
- Win the end of the day (with a gentle transition and the right question), and you win the whole night.

7

Master Your Mind by Mastering the Voices in Your Head

Acknowledgment:
We owe a huge debt of gratitude to three individuals for teaching us about influencing the voices in our own heads. First is Dr. Shad Helmstetter, specifically his groundbreaking book *What to Say When You Talk to Yourself*. It made us actually understand that "positive affirmations" are not simply material for a *Saturday Night Live* sketch – it's the most direct path to rewiring your brain and unlocking almost anything you want from life. Second is Ed Foreman, whose Successful Life Course has benefited hundreds of thousands of leaders, including us. Third is John Assaraf, founder of NeuroGym and author of *The Answer*. *The Answer* taught us about what we call targeted affirmations, which have helped our clients manifest incredible results almost on command. Anything you can buy or read from these titans will make your life better.

Your Brain Is Talking to You

That's right, whether you knew it or not *your brain is talking to you* right now, and all the time. The quality and the intentionality of that conversation that you're always having with yourself is ultimately the most influential input source of all. In the last chapter you learned about a number of different input sources for programming your mind. Every single one of them filters into this one – your self-talk, a.k.a. your "internal dialogue." The conversation with yourself is happening constantly, whether you're aware of it or not. It's always there, and it's inside of you – so it's always influencing you.

Fortunately, your internal dialogue is not just the most *influential* input source, it's also one of the most *influence-able* (if that's actually a word). Because it's always working on you, you can always be working on it, and the shifts you make will start rewiring your brain both immediately and long term. This is another place where the 2 mm principle is in full effect. Small upgrades here can make a universe of difference.

Case Study: 5 Star Insurance

One of our favorite case studies is the team at 5 Star Insurance Group in Wisconsin. When we met owner Patti-Jo Toellner and her top salesperson Staci Evans, they were:

1. Doing an absolutely amazing job of taking care of their clients (which they'd always done and continue to do).
2. Doing what they would call a "good job" of hitting their goals/running a profitable agency.

This sounds great, right? But the flip side was that they were:

1. Driving each other crazy.
2. Exhausted and worn down physically and mentally, to the point of literally being hospitalized. Especially after the Annual Enrollment Period for health insurance, which to an insurance agency like 5 Star is like tax season for an accountant, both Patti-Jo and Staci would tell you that they were pretty much a train wreck.

3. As a result of 1 and 2, not able to maximize their potential and grow the way they really wanted to.

When we started working with them in coaching, it became glaringly obvious that they needed two things:

1. It was critical that they upgrade their time management to avoid being run ragged by the sheer "busy-ness" of dealing with thousands of clients in a six-week stretch. The two-hour solution was a miracle for them.
2. They needed to heal their relationship with each other, which had to begin with healing their respective relationships with themselves. Both of them had some significant growing that they needed to experience, and so we started with how they were talking to themselves.

With the rest of this chapter we'll detail the upgrades they used, but you'll want to know the results first. A year after the work they did with us, it was a much different story at 5 Star. Of course they were still doing an incredible job of caring for their clients (that will never change, nor should it), but they had an entirely different experience.

- 5 Star Insurance absolutely soared. They crushed goals and had their best year ever by every measure.
- During the Annual Enrollment Period, they worked hard but almost totally avoided feeling overwhelmed, backed up, or stressed. The result was that they actually took the most stressful time of the year and felt energized and satisfied all the way through. They made it look easy.
- The vibe in the office is now a thing of beauty. Patti-Jo and Staci now can't shut up about how much they *love* each other and their team. The team has grown dramatically in both head count and quality, because people are just beating down their door to be part of the culture.
- Both of them have developed a "Money Magnet" that is really impressive. They're consistently making new sales and generating revenue even during the times where

traditionally there's nothing happening. The experience of money flowing to them from both known and unknown sources is an everyday occurrence.

Doesn't that sound pleasant? We see results like this with nearly all our coaching clients, and it comes from the intentional use of affirmations.

What's an "affirmation"? Are we talking about Stuart Smalley: "I'm good enough, I'm smart enough, and doggone-it, people like me"?

Something like this . . . just less cheesy. An affirmation is simply a short sentence that describes or affirms something that you want to be, do, or have. They're typically written as statements (as opposed to questions) in the present tense (as opposed to the future tense) and in the first person. Some people call them "I am" statements.

Total Lunatic or Sales Genius?

From Roger:

My first exposure to affirmations was when I sold books with the Southwestern Company . . . and quite frankly I thought it was just plain nuts at first. The sales, leadership, and life training were world-class, but when they started talking about "saying positive phrases out loud," I just thought, well, that's weird. The company wanted me to:

- Wake up in the morning and say "It's gonna be a great day!"
- Verbally exclaim "I feel happy, healthy, and terrific!" throughout the day.
- Affirm "This is good, great, and wonderful and here's three reasons why," anytime something went wrong.

I definitely thought I was too cool for it. And like a dummy I actually rejected the practice entirely, until I spent a day with Don Meyer. Don was the first really great mentor I ever had, and he happened to be the number-one salesperson in the company. I spent a day watching him work, which turned out to be one of the most valuable learning experiences of my life. There were two things that really stood out in his methods.

First, *everybody* bought from Don. He made a customer out of every single person we sat down with that day, and he sold more on Monday than I had sold in any prior week.

Second, he never stopped talking to himself. All day long, in between calls, he was constantly saying things like:

"I feel happy, healthy, and terrific."

"I'm in tune, I'm in touch, I'm on top."

"I love people and I love my job."

And then my personal favorite: "Everyone loves me, and everyone buys from me. Everybody's gettin' 'em!"

I seriously thought *What kind of nut job does this?* until it hit me that *everything he was saying to himself was actually coming true*, right in front of my eyes. Especially the part about how "Everyone buys from me." So my mind began to open.

Later that year, Don gave me a copy of the book *What to Say When You Talk to Yourself*, and my whole picture changed. Written in 1981, it explained some of the then-budding field of neuroscience, and how what you say to yourself physically rewires your brain to make those statements become reality. I finally bought into this "positive phrases thing" . . . and what was the very next thing that happened?

My income tripled. You can probably imagine, that was enough to make me a full-on convert. Fast-forward 20 years to when we started coaching top-performing sales professionals and business leaders, and we can say that it was a well-designed system of handcrafted affirmations that become a bedrock foundation of the work we do. Here are the fundamentals of your system for mastering your own self-talk.

The Basic Premise: You've Gotta Be Working on It

Again, to be clear, your brain is always talking to you, and the quality of that dialogue is a major determinant of where your mind focuses, and thereby the quality of your life. Like all of your other input sources, there are only two options for what your self-talk can do. *Neutral* is not an option—your self-talk will either be positive, uplifting, and helpful *or* it will be negative, draining, and destructive. Because of your default settings, the tendency will be for your self-talk to be more negative, *unless you are intentionally working on it.*

Happily, working on your self-talk requires zero investment of time, because it's already happening. *Working on it* means that you simply take advantage of both your reactive opportunities (where something happens and you're responding) and your proactive opportunities (where you're making it happen of your own volition) to notice and then guide the conversation that you're having with yourself.

You Know These Two Things Will Happen

Let's talk about the *reactive* opportunities first. There are two things that you can know with certainty will happen every single day.

1. You Will Wake Up

Every morning, you wake up . . . until you don't, at which point all of this becomes irrelevant. You've not reached that point yet, so let's just revisit a key tactic that you may have missed earlier.

That microscopically brief moment right when your eyes open and you become conscious is where you have the most theta brainwaves of your whole day, which makes it the most opportune moment of the whole day for programming. That moment can pass unnoticed (it does for the majority of people) *or* you can plant a wonderful seed and declare:

This is gonna be a great day.

Sounds too simple, right? Starting your day with that phrase takes approximately 1.5 seconds (we actually timed it), but don't be fooled. That 1.5 seconds sets your brain off on exactly the right note for the day and helps your subconscious Elephant move toward a "great day" all day long.

Can you vary the exact phrase? Of course – one of our top coaches, Penn Vieau, says "Something amazing is gonna happen to me today." We've had clients use different variations like:

- "Thanks for another day!"
- Psalm 118:24: "This is the day that the Lord has made, let us rejoice and be glad in it."
- "Big day today!"
- "I'm so lucky!"

So feel free to experiment with your morning saying – what you say is not as important as the timing. You know you're going to wake up one way or the other, so why not wake up and master your mind in the process?

2. You'll Be Asked the Most Frequently Asked Question in the World:

How are you?

In every language, that's the question that gets asked most often. Think about how often you get asked this question or ask it of someone else. Five times a day? Ten? You probably respond to this question several times a day, and in the majority of cases, the response is unconscious and mediocre at best.

Fine, how are you?

Do you want to master your mind? Don't miss the easy stuff! Have an answer for this question that's intentional and positive. Ed Foreman taught us to always answer that question with an enthusiastic "Terrific!" and we use that answer to this day. We know, it doesn't sound like it should make that much of a difference, but it does.

The first time you get asked how you're doing, and you say "Terrific!," do you know what happens? Right: You actually feel terrific for a few seconds, which results in the beginning of a neural pathway that wires in "feeling terrific." One time doesn't really make much difference, but 5 or 10 times per day? It starts to add up, and you notice yourself feeling terrific more and more consistently. You mastered your mind for more positive energy, you made yourself much more attractive in every sense, *and it took exactly zero time.*

Just your reactive opportunities for improved self-talk can make a gigantic difference. Making proactive upgrades is where you can make some real magic happen.

And Then You Can Make Some Things Happen

Our clients usually see the biggest jumps in their results when we help them handcraft their system for proactively using positive affirmations to upgrade their self-talk. "Proactive" in this case just means that you initiate it, rather than acting in response to another person or situation. What we and our clients do is simply carve out two to five minutes (that's all it takes) to read their own custom, handwritten, targeted words of affirmation. They generally do this twice a day, occasionally more.

1. Craft 10–20 Affirmations

The crux of the process and the biggest time commitment lies in the actual construction of a set of affirmations. We spend lots of time with our coaching clients in this stage. Doing this well is worth investing time and money . . . it's a big part of how we earn our Cheerios! We can give you the essentials right here. There are endless possibilities – for example, simply google "list of affirmations" and see what comes up, or better yet, read *What to Say When You Talk to Yourself* – it's still a definitive work.

Some affirmations can be more general, universal, or what we call *foundational.* Some of our own personal foundational affirmations are the following:

- "I love people and I love my business!"
- "Day by day, in every way, I'm getting better and better!" This is the original affirmation, developed in the 1800s by Dr. Emile Coue – google it, the story is fascinating.
- "I constantly feel God and His Universe caring for me and lining things up perfectly!"

A little secret sauce: Some of your affirmations should be *targeted*. *Targeted* means that they address a specific area where you want results, and sometimes even quantify those results. Some targeted affirmations that our clients love are:

- "My business grows elegantly and effortlessly, by at least 20% annually."
- "Money flows to me from both known and unknown sources."
- "I maintain my ideal weight of 170, because I eat well and consistently exercise."
- "I am a money magnet"
- "I'm super-focused and fully present in all I do. As a result, I'm incredibly productive."

You want a mix of foundational and targeted affirmations, in a list of 10–20 in all. Helping our clients craft affirmations that pinpoint the results they want is our specialty, so please reach out to our team if you could use some guidance. We'll have to charge you, but it'll be worth every penny.

2. *Write 'Em Out*

The next step is to write your 10–20 affirmations out. Do not type them—*write them out* by hand. The most effective way we've found is on a set of 3-by-5 notecards. Yes, it takes a little time, but that's perfect. Slowing down is speeding up, right? Handwrite one affirmation per card, so that you end up with a stack of cards, like flashcards.

3. Carry 'Em with You Everywhere

You've now got a stack of cards full of pure gold. Put a rubber band around that stack, or find something to serve as a case, and put it in your pocket. Carry that stack around with you. You can bust it out and flip through it when you have a spare moment, and even if you never do, there's still value in carrying the cards with you. In the worst-case scenario, you've got a physical reminder of *what* you want and *why* you want it that travels with you like a steadfast little buddy.

4. Set Aside a Few Minutes Each Morning and Evening

The last piece of the affirmation process is to intentionally let your own words of affirmation saturate your mind a couple of times each day. It's really simple . . . just pull out your stack, and read the cards to yourself, one by one. Take your time – even if you go slowly and read each one twice, it'll still only take two to three minutes to read 10–20 cards. Do this twice a day, once early in the morning and once as you're winding down at night (alpha and theta brain wave times, remember?).

And that's it! You can be as creative as you want, but creativity is not necessary. You can read your cards silently or out loud. You can do it straight or use silly accents. You can decorate your cards with glitter or keep them plain and simple. You can add a midday reading of your cards (often helpful), but it's not required. We'd definitely recommend making your affirmation flashcards part of your two-hour solution, but again it's not a requirement.

By using these four steps, even in their bare-bones state, you'll notice a difference in your energy and your confidence within a few days. If you read them consistently for a few weeks, you'll have a new and wildly effective habit on your hands. And if you practice your affirmations consistently for 90 days (especially if you've enlisted the accountability of a coach), you will have mastered your mind in a way that truly transforms you.

Enjoy.

Chapter Review

- Your "self-talk" – the conversation you're constantly having with yourself – is ultimately the most influential input source for your mind.
- You have the ability – in fact, the responsibility – to influence this influencer.
- You can influence your self-talk both reactively and proactively, and it takes very little time
- We teach the integrated process our clients use to upgrade their self-talk, and thereby their results.

8

Master Your Mind with the Ridiculous Power of *Clarity*

Frankly my dear, I just don't give a damn!

—*Rhett Butler*, *Gone With the Wind*

You may have gathered from Chapter 2 (where you learned about your subconscious Elephant) that your brain benefits from *clarity* about *what* you want and *why* you want that more than pretty much anything else. In this chapter you'll learn about how to develop clarity for yourself.

Shameless plug for our coaching: *If* you find yourself struggling to get clear about your aims, please reach out to us or our team. Having someone work with you on the issue of clarity can be worth its weight in gold.

The Power of Not Caring

While attending a sales training conference for financial advisors a few years back, the topic turned to communicating one's "differentiator" to their client(s). We went around the room and ironically 70 percent of the guys (yes, this industry is still basically a good old boy's club, and the women who have accepted that this is the current paradigm are figuring out ways to really effectively differentiate) had the exact same answers: "I love to help people" or "I take care of my clients" or "I listen." Then there was Don.

"Oh, that's easy. I have the power of not caring."

Mi-i-ind. Blo-o-o-w-w-wn.

For about three months after that, we ended up having countless conversations with people about this concept, and the common theme was this: The most relaxed, happy, and productive people we talked to all shared with us that they had basically stopped caring about things that didn't matter.

Now to be clear, they all shared that they still had plenty to care about or be concerned with or accountable for in their lives. But notice what they were not concerned with: anything that did not directly impact their big picture (see Figure 8.1). In other words, they had *clarity*.

Figure 8.1 Not Caring Brings Clarity

Elephants Like Clear Pictures

Countless clients have shared over the years that the number-one benefit of going through coaching is the amount of clarity that they gain. Clarity in what they believe in and stand for, clarity on what's important to them, clarity in what they are working on and when they are working on it, clarity in being present in everything they do. And clarity in their decision-making process. We are always amazed at the kinds of things that are priorities to people before they gain clarity, and then how little those things come up in conversation later on down the road.

As you learned in Chapter 2, your Elephant needs clarity in order to effectively get you the results you are looking for. Having a clear picture of *what* you want and *why* it is most important to you is arguably the single biggest factor in getting your brain to work for you instead of against you. It's what gets your Elephant to say, "Okay, lemme go get that for you," and at the same time, it gets your Ant out of the way so that your subconscious can go to work uninterrupted. If being able to let go of your conscious thoughts and beliefs is one of the first steps to this, then harnessing the power of not caring is like when you bend your knee to lift your leg. It's the first piece of the puzzle.

The "power of not caring" does a couple of things for you. First, it helps keep you off the emotional roller-coaster of life. When you spend less time thinking about, worrying about, and generally being concerned with the things that aren't a bother, it frees your mind to be able to focus on the things you *do* care about. You eliminate any creative roadblocks that arise due to structured or negative thinking. You approach situations with more clarity, less concern, and less skepticism, and answer questions with more confidence, and operate with more energy.

Energy Suckers Need Not Apply

One of the biggest roadblocks in the way of progress or results or success or whatever you want to call it is an overabundance of negative influence around you, both directly and indirectly. As you learned in Chapter 3, one of your brain's *un*helpful default settings is its tendency to focus on and gravitate toward negativity. Any time your brain sees or hears anything that it can perceive as negative, the quick blink response is to agree and help pile it on. When that happens, it's imperative to *slow down* and notice what is happening. Notice whether what is happening can be categorized as positive or negative. Think about whether hopping on the bandwagon will move you closer to or further from your goals/vision. Is agreeing with the situation allowing you to live your purpose? This seems like a lot to think about, but I guarantee, it takes about three seconds to execute, and those could be three of the most important seconds of your day.

An often overlooked benefit of the power of not caring is that this approach can and often will help weed out these negative influences in your life. Have you ever noticed that people who like to complain are always looking for someone to share their complaints with? Not sure what I mean? Go hop in line for anything and listen to people around you. Listen to how many people want to drag you into their personal hell. Folks like this have a couple of names – "energy suckers" is my favorite. But as hard as they try to get you into their pity party, nothing turns them off faster than simply *not* acknowledging their problems. With practice, operating in this zone will put up a force field and energy suckers will avoid you. This is sort of similar to the way dogs sense fear, but in reverse.

You may be saying to yourself, "That sounds mean!" or "But I'm really understanding and sympathetic, and I like to help people." That is all well and good, but understand that you can still help people while not caring about their issues. Here's how . . . let's say you have a friend who is dealing with a non-issue. That friend comes to you "for advice" (which usually means to unload on you). The part of you that expresses "I really care about you" sits there and listens and wonders how long this tirade is going to last (on average it's about seven to eight minutes). At the end of their filibuster, what have you gained? Nothing! To truly "help out," might it be more productive to stop that person in their tracks and offer them the nice dose of perspective they may have missed due to their current outlook? Like a gambler who's convinced that one more hand is all it takes to get out of the hole, a complainer feels like one more set of ears hearing this is all they need to get over it. And I can tell you that is NEVER the case. Plus, stopping that conversation early gives you your valuable seven minutes back. *Score!* In the event you couldn't pull the e-brake in time, one of my favorite lines for ending conversations is, "Well, that's definitely one way to look at it!" and then turning the conversation toward something different.

Lessen the Caring Load

So how do you start not caring? Here are a couple of tips:

- As you can imagine from reading this chapter, the first thing you need to do is to be hyper clear about what *is* important to you. We said at the beginning that the most successful people don't get hung up on anything that doesn't directly impact their big picture. In order to determine what will and what won't impact your big picture, you *need to have a big picture*. Be operating from a place where your core values, purpose, and vision are front and center. What does that mean? Start your day by reviewing your core values, purpose, vision, and goals. Every. Day. This is the quickest, easiest, and cheapest way to refocus your brain in a way that "feeds your elephant" and gets it moving in the right direction. After all, getting an elephant on a mission to change directions or stop takes a heck of a lot of effort. Just like the principle of inertia: An object in motion stays in motion and an object at rest stays at rest . . . unless that object is acted upon by an outside force. Thoughts, while internal, act like an outside force in this scenario, so get them to work for you in getting your elephant moving and generating momentum. Or to get it to *stop* moving in a direction that isn't getting you toward your goals. Now, if you don't have your core values, purpose, vision, or goals defined, that is where you start. I guarantee things will get *lots* easier for you once you have those things identified. (For help in identifying core values, purpose, and vision, refer to *Train Your Brain For Success*.)

- In any situation, opportunity, or potential distraction, ask yourself "Is there anything more important to me right now than this?" If you can think of even one thing that you would rather be doing or that is more important than what you are currently engaged in, stop caring about doing what you are doing and get back on track.
- Only engage with people and activities that propel you. When you spend more time with energy fillers instead of energy suckers, you will form new behavioral habits. More often than not, a byproduct of new habits is the lack of desire to be surrounded by people or activities that drag you down. See what happens here? By focusing only on the things and people you care about, you end up "not caring" about anything else. And that thought process gains momentum *really* quickly.

With time and practice, the power of not caring will help elevate you mentally and remove energy-draining people and events from your life. But remember, this is not the power of being a jerk. The power of not caring does not give you permission to be a dismissive, self-centered a-hole. Slow down and remember to accept that some folks simply haven't learned how to use this power yet.

Be Too ______

From Robb: A few years back, I had a phone meeting with a colleague and our weekly call took an interesting turn. We had been talking about the usual – goals and tasks, opportunities and challenges, wins and losses – when the topic turned to the concept of being too ___. This could mean too preoccupied to do such and such, or too depressed to go out, or too cash-strapped to book the flight or too uninterested to pick up the phone or too tired to work out in the morning. Or just too busy in general.

This got me thinking. How many times have you asked someone how they have been and the first words out of their mouth are "Busy!"? I think people have just started believing that busy is the new normal.

People hide behind busy. They use busy as an excuse to not accomplish what they want to. Busy gets in the way of success, it gets in the way of making good decisions, and it can be energy draining. Busyness also begets more busyness, leading to a vicious cycle of stress, strain, and unhappiness.

But what if there were a way to make busy work for you. What if busy was a good thing? And then it dawned on me. There's a flip side to busy.

We had a pretty good list of excuses made up, and then I asked her, "What if you were just too busy to believe all that B.S.?"

Silence.

I love this question. One of my core values is *perspective*, and I am always looking for a different perspective on things. I ask myself "What are you too ___ for?" a lot, and aside from initially framing my day, this is probably the second most effective way to get myself back on track when I am off or not crystal clear. It is a question that can keep you on task when it is so easy to make excuses and get off task.

There's always "the story," and too often people leave it at that. Where they miss out on making great things happen is figuring out the flip side of the "blank."

- What if I were too busy to chase people down for money? (Fun fact, *every* time I stop calling, they send it.)
- What if I were too busy to listen to excuses? (The quicker I hang up, the sooner I can talk to the next prospect.)
- What if I were too successful to worry about what it means to be successful? (Who cares, as long as you are happy?)

The idea of being "too busy to ____" comes up *all* the time. I hear it from prospects, from coworkers, from family members, and sometimes from myself! The brain naturally wants to focus on the negative, and it is really easy to get comfortable sitting in the "too ___" state. The next time you find yourself making an excuse, think about what it would take for that excuse never to have the opportunity to arise. In addition to the above, here are some fun ones we came up with:

- Too busy to overeat.
- Too focused on the big picture to get concerned with the little bumps along the way.
- Too committed to excellence to leave the bank before the alarm gets set. (Thanks, Lisa!)
- Too dedicated to family time to check my email.
- Too punctual to squeeze that one last call in.
- Too committed to writing my book to turn on the TV. (Yep, I had to remind myself of this one a few times in getting this baby to print.)

What are you "too ___" for? Make a list. What challenges are you faced with in your day to day life? Too busy? Too stretched thin? Too broke? Too stressed? Too fat? Too lazy? Now identify what is in the way of you doing what you want. Then find the reverse and focus on *that*. That's the flip side of busy. The following is an example.

A booking agent at our company (the individuals who do a lot of the initial outreach to prospective clients) was afraid of "bothering" the managing partners of the firms we were trying to work with. Since they all talked internally, she was too afraid to follow up more than four times or be direct with them to get them to schedule a call with us. As a result, her production levels plummeted (along with her compensation).

After a few one-on-one chats, she realized that that these prospects were inundated with calls like hers and that they were in fact bothered by people who were yammering on and on and wasting their time trying to be "sell-y." With this newfound awareness, she decided she was too dedicated to helping improve efficiency to be afraid of bothering them. Her outlook changed. Her tone changed. Her dialogue changed. Her results changed. Her income changed. What didn't change was the script she followed to get these folks to take our calls. What she did do was make a decision on what she was committed to and how she could best offer that to these "busy" people.

End result, "I'm too focused on efficiency to be afraid of hearing no."

Clarity in what you are chasing down and its importance to you is the first step in living an effective, easy, mind-mastered life. The second step is using that clarity to identify what you are doing and when you are doing it. Which leads us to our next chapter . . .

Chapter Review

- Quit caring so much.
- Have a clear picture for what is important to you. Stay focused on it.
- Learn how to be too ___.

9

Master Your Mind by Mastering Your Week: The Two-Hour Solution

If you're not running your week, your week is running you . . . and that's no fun at all.

—*Robb Zbierski, bestselling author*

Busy versus Productive

When I met Aubrey, she was a woman on a mission. And she was a bundle of busyness. She had purchased an independent insurance agency a few years before from the gentleman who had given her her first job in insurance. She started off as an administrative assistant and had worked her way up to the point where she was running the business for the agent who had hired her, as he transitioned into retirement. Like any smart businessman, he decided to get out of the way and sell the whole agency to her so she could continue to grow the business.

Aubrey was also a very active member of her industry association. She attended monthly meetings at both the local and statewide levels. As part of her involvement, she spearheaded the internal leadership training program and was responsible for recruiting, selling, and delivering a year-long curriculum to her peers who enrolled in the program.

As if her work life weren't busy enough, Aubrey also had (well, she still has) a passion for crocheting and sold small projects through her Etsy store. She was involved in leadership on her neighborhood association, holding both board positions and chairing an annual art festival and holiday fundraiser. Oh, wait, did I mention she had just graduated to a black belt in Jiu Jitsu and helped teach classes in the dojo, where not only was she continuously training herself, but she was also helping train others who were on their martial arts journey? Yeah . . . she had a few things on her plate, but the biggest thing on her plate was growing and sustaining her insurance business.

When Aubrey took over, there were six massive vertical filing cabinets filled with decades of client files. Some new, some old, some current, but many either outdated or *really* outdated (as in, they passed away). She came to our first call convinced that if she spent an hour a day going through and following up with these old clients she was going to make enough money to hit her income goal.

While Aubrey had a ton going on externally (some of it working against her), she had one major theme going on internally that was working for her. Through her work as a facilitator for the leadership training, she had started down the path of gaining clarity on the things that were important to her. She had taken the time to reflect on who she was and what she stood for and what she wanted to achieve. This proved to be one of the most valuable things she brought to our sessions.

After a few weeks of "baseline" training and curriculum, it came time to learn about and lay out the Two-Hour Solution. This is where things started to get fun . . .

If you already read *Train Your Brain for Success*, you know from Chapter 11 what the Two-Hour Solution is and how to use it. For anyone reading this book who might not be aware of the Two-Hour Solution, next is a synopsis.

The Pillar of Brain-Friendly Time Management: The Two-Hour Solution

The 2-Hour Solution is a proven seven-step process for effective time management. It is a weekly meeting that you have with yourself. The purpose of this meeting is to get reconnected with the things that mean the most to you, to review your big-picture vision, dreams, and goals and schedule your next one or two weeks in a way that will help you achieve your goals and vision. You may have figured this out already, but it should be about a two-hour chunk of time that you dedicate to this meeting. Now understand, this is *not* a time to create your task list. It is a time that allows you to gain clarity on what you want to accomplish, set intentions for the week, and practice visualizing getting what you want out of your days. In a nutshell, it's designed to allow you to run your life instead of your life running you. I mentioned that this is a seven-step process – here they are, in order of priority:

Step 1: Spend time getting reconnected with your core values, purpose, vision, and goals

See the life you are hoping to live. See how you want to carry yourself in situations. Act like you have been there before! Remember the level of excitement you had when you identified these crucial pieces. There is a reason that this is the first step. Without a clear goal, it doesn't matter what you do with the rest of the week. If you don't have a clear intention for what you want to accomplish in your meetings, it doesn't matter what you discuss in those meetings. Without a great understanding of where you are trying to get, you might take *any* way to get there, and it probably won't be the fastest, most direct, or even the easiest path. For a lot of the folks we work with, this step constitutes 30–40 minutes of that two-hour chunk of time. Just like a prize-winning boxer walking in to music and pyrotechnics to pump him/herself up, spend time getting yourself energized to take on your week by visualizing the life you are chasing down! Just don't light the office on fire . . .

Refreshers Always Help

Dan went through our curriculum and gained some incredible insights into what was most important to him and how he could use his professional skills to benefit folks in his personal life. After wrapping up coaching with us, Dan was out on his own and quickly moved up the corporate ladder, earning a promotion he had been chasing for three years. Talk about payoff! However, he quickly realized that with more salary and title comes more responsibility and work. Dan called us out of the blue one day to say thanks. When asked why he felt the need to take time out of his now busier day to tell us this, his answer was simple and poignant:

> "You made me review all these important things like core values and purpose and vision every day and every week. It got burned into my brain. In this new role, I am faced with all kinds of new challenges, decisions, and situations. It's a real grind some days, and I'll be honest, there have been more than a few occasions where I have thought about either quitting or stepping back into my old role. But then I find my vision statement and I take a few minutes to get reconnected with it and everything that's important to me. It's almost spooky how every time I get done reading through it and remembering when we created it that I am instantly motivated to get back at it. And it's so much easier to make decisions from that place mentally."

Not bad, Dan . . . not bad at all.

Step 2: Schedule Your Commitments

These are the things that will *not* fall off the calendar, no matter what. Getting married on Saturday? Definitely counts as a commitment in my book! Having a scheduled C-section on Wednesday? Probably happening no matter what. Let's get that chunk of time carved out for you. Taking your children to the zoo on Thursday? Same idea. The good news is that *most* of the people we know already use some type of scheduling device and commitments typically already live on the calendar, just by virtue of said individual being a functional, responsible, commonsensical human being. This is a great time to really reflect on whether or not that event is in fact a commitment, or if there is something with greater importance that needs to happen during that time. To repeat . . . we want to move from reactive to proactive in how you approach your week.

Step 3: Schedule Your Excellence Time

This is the time/these are the activities that make you better/stronger/smarter/faster. Do you like to work out? Get it carved out on the calendar. Studying for your Series 65? When are you going to commit to reading and studying? Need continuing education to maintain your licensure? What conventions or workshops will you be attending? Other things that fall under the Excellence Time umbrella include reading and listening to audio programs, watching any training or inspirational/educational videos, meditation, runs, bike rides, weight lifting, yoga . . . you get the picture. Like I said, a direct result of these activities it that they make you a better version of you. Now a lot of people question why "going for a walk in the morning" needs to get put on the calendar at all, or why it gets put on the calendar before your "work stuff." It's fundamentally for two reasons: First, these are the activities that if not scheduled, get *really* easy to skip if something else comes up.

From Robb: For instance, working from home allows me the freedom to go for a lunchtime bike ride any day I want to. But the opportunist DNA in me wants to do as much work as I can, and lunchtime for me isn't lunchtime for potential clients in other parts of the country. Unless I have my rides on my calendar, it's easy for me to make one more call or pick up the phone when it rings or reply to that email that could probably wait till my red time (more on that in a minute), which happens in the early part of my afternoon, after the ride.

Second, since these are the things that make you a better you, it's imperative that they get done/accomplished in order for you to be on top of your game. They are not unlike if/when the oxygen masks drop from the ceiling of the plane. Secure your mask before helping others. Do you know why they include that reminder on every single flight? It's because people *love* to help other people. They will go out of their way to help people. But you can't help someone when you are dead. You need oxygen in order to function. Think of Excellence Time as your personal oxygen mask.

Step 4: *Schedule Your Green Time*

It's called Green Time because green is the color of money (or grass, if you are working with landscape architects, as we were a few years back). These are the activities that directly put money in your pocket. This is when financial advisors are available for client meetings. Or when Oral Surgeons are scheduled to be in surgery. Realtors, this is when you are available to write offers. Mortgage lenders, this is when you are available to meet with potential clients. Not sure what constitutes Green Time? It's anything that is listed in your job description (except "Other Duties As Assigned" – that's just an HR addition).

Notice I used the term *when you are available*. The Two-Hour Solution is what helps most of our clients transition from a reactive approach to their business (and life) to a proactive one. For extra credit, set your intention for your Green Time meetings. Really flex your visualization muscles and start to see what you want to accomplish. See the reaction on your client's or patient's face when you are all finished up.

Moving from Sell-y to Tell-y, Thanks to Green Time

A life insurance agent we were working with was hesitant to set specific times when she would make herself available to follow up with clients. In her words, "I want to be available when my client is available to meet. I don't want to chase them down sounding all *sell-y* about wanting to close the loop." Unsurprisingly, she spent more time chasing down applicants than she did meeting with new prospects.

After a few frustrating months of this, she finally embraced the concept of scheduling specific Green Time chunks twice every week. Any applications that came in between her two times got moved to the next time for follow-up. If the client wasn't available at the next chunk, they were then moved to the one after that. What changed? She stopped being a slave to others' calendars. She decided that *telling* people when she was available to follow up was more effective. There were dedicated times that she set up for the purpose of assisting new clients.

As a result, she had *way* more time for prospecting and generating new business. Plus her clients really appreciated the consistency in her calendar!

Step 5: Schedule Your Red Time

Red Time is the time you proactively dedicate to accomplishing the tasks that need to get done in order for you to have Green Time; however, they do not directly put money in your pocket. Examples of Red Time include (but are not limited to): submitting an application, any client meeting at which you are gathering information or presenting a plan, team or staff meetings, driving to an appointment, showing a home, calling to prep a client for their speech, and picking the kids up from school. Notice a common theme? *All* of these things need to get done in order for you to maximize your Green Time activities. As a matter of fact, if this time and these activities didn't exist on your calendar, you'd probably be out of a job in no time as you would spend all your time and energy on remedial tasks. Ever had one of those hamster wheel days? You know, the one where you work and work and work all day but you ever feel as though you made any progress? Chances are very good that those days are consumed with Red Time activities.

Step 6: *Schedule or Notice Your Flex Time*

Once you have Commitments, Excellence Time, Green Time, and Red Time carved out, you should start to see some holes or windows in your calendar. This is Flex Time. Flex Time allows you to use the five most powerful words in productivity:

"Love to… can't right now."

Ever had a client or someone in your life who needed your help *right now* and needed it done *right now* and expected you to drop everything you were working on in order to them them *right now*? Yeah, that's when "Love to . . . can't right now" starts to come in handy. Rather than letting your hour/day/week explode right in front of you, try busting out that line. But you can use it *only* if you have dedicated time (Flex Time) set aside to help out with stuff like that. Because here's the deal. When you tell someone "Love to . . . can't right now. But I can help you at 2 p.m. today," one of two things is going to happen. Either they will come back at 2 p.m., or they will figure it out on their own, giving you *more time*! Alternatively, if the boss comes up to you and says, hey, I need this and I need it *now*, Flex Time allows you to shift what you were working on in that moment to that Flex Time later in the day or the week, allowing you to get both things accomplished. Pretty sweet, huh?

Paid by the Minute: A Case Study in Saying No

Here's one of my favorite examples (and for some folks it is extreme, but stay with me here) of putting this whole system to use. James is one of the premier periodontists in the country. He's a bell cow: Other periodontists will follow what he does in an effort to replicate his success. Other periodontists will go to him to have their periodontal work done. I was having a conversation with James and a few of our friends a few years ago and the topic of availability came up. He shared this with me:

> My team is really motivated by compensation. We have a bonus structure in place and ultimately the whole thing is tied to my ability to be in the operating room, doing the procedures that our patients come to us for. I also get asked to lecture and travel from time to time, and I have a family that I love being with. So my time in the office is (A) extremely limited and (B) extremely valuable. I have done the math and figured out that when I am doing my money-making activities (in the operating room, running patient consultations, follow-ups, et cetera) I'm contributing to the practice at a rate of $1,600 per hour. My team knows if I do well, they do well. The less time I have to get involved with things they can handle, the better the office does. You have to make them understand that it is all right to make a mistake.
>
> My team very much wants to make sure that we are profitable, but they often feel the need to come to me with questions or to ask my opinion on something. Needless to say, this cuts into my available time to do my money-making activities. So I have empowered them to make their own decisions by declaring the following: If you have a question or an idea that is worth more than $1,600 per hour, absolutely approach me with it. I'm happy to help out. If, however, your question or idea is not worth $1,600 per hour you have my permission to figure it out on your own. Come to me when it is worth at least $1,600 per hour."

I had been sharing this story with groups all over the country and it was really hitting home and illustrating the point of valuing your time. So you can imagine my surprise when I was at dinner with James a few months later, and I was thanking him for sharing this story and approach when he replied:

"Oh, yeah . . . we don't do that anymore."

"What? Why? What happened?"

"I'm now at $27 per minute. I had too many people stopping to interrupt my flow with questions that started out 'Doctor, I just need a quick minute of your time . . .' So I broke down the rate and told my staff, 'If you have a question or an idea that is worth more than $27 per minute, absolutely approach me with it. I'm happy to help out. If, however, your question or idea is not worth $27 per minute you have my permission to figure it out on your own. Come to me when it is worth at least $27 per minute.' My current rules are to come to me if your decision could ruin a referral relationship, cause you or a patient physical harm, or cost the office over $700. Otherwise it is probably not worth $27 per minute!"

I was entertained by this update until I asked a follow-up question, "And how is that working out for you and your staff?"

James didn't even hesitate, "Robb, we had a record year, I was able to bonus out my team members more than I ever have. And they earned every dollar of it."

At that point I was just in awe.

Step 7: *Schedule Your Recreation Time*

This is the time you dedicate to doing whatever you do to rest or recharge the battery. This is date night, this is movie night, this is when you work on your crafting, this is when you work on your yard or in your garden. These are the activities that bring you joy and renewal. Yes, this can even be a trashy TV night, if that is what you are into.

As you are setting and reviewing all these different time blocks, the most important thing to do is to take a moment to set an intention for these activities. It's the secret sauce that makes this whole exercise work. Visualize that prospect signing the paperwork or the patient seeing their new smile for the first time. See your child giving you a huge hug after you took him or her to lunch unannounced. In order to really "feed your Elephant," you need to spend time creating crystal-clear pictures of the actions you are going to take and the goals you are looking to achieve.

Case Study: Turning Down Time into Green Time

From Robb: Not long after we moved to Illinois, I was bored. It was mid January (the most depressing week of the year) and we had been cooped up for months. I had put on plenty of winter weight, the indoor training definitely wasn't calling my name, I wasn't able to ride outside, and I needed something to do. As a hobby, I always enjoyed working on, fixing, and tuning-up bicycles. Whenever I had down time, I often found myself in the workshop tinkering with my bikes. Well, all my personal bikes were dialed in, so I thought it might be helpful to offer my services to the neighborhood I live in. My neighborhood sits smack-dab in the middle of walking/riding distance to four schools, three public pools and two grocery stores. It's a suburban parent's dream!

The closest bike shops were at least a 10- to 15-minute drive away, so why not offer a repair and service business out of my garage? After all, people love to support their neighbors, right? As a way to stand out, I decided I would let people offset the cost of their service with beer. Hence, Beers for Gears was born. A Craigslist ad and a Facebook page were created to let people know I was in business.

I was cautiously optimistic this would be a good idea and well received, but I also knew that I did *not* want to be at other peoples' beck and call every minute of every day. In order for this to work, I could only take appointments on a schedule that worked for me, so I found a scheduling program that tied into my Google calendar (www.timetrade.com). It allowed me to set up specific days of the week and times of the day where I would be available to take one-hour appointments. Making it even sweeter, those appointments would only show up if I wasn't already marked as "busy" on my Google calendar.

Having been practicing the Two-Hour Solution for a few years, I had noticed certain days and times when I was available (i.e., Fridays after 3 p.m. and Sundays after 2 p.m.). And then I knew that the kids went to bed at 7 p.m. every night, leaving me at least two hours of "down time." So between trends in availability during the day, coupled with wide-open evenings after 7 every night, I found 15 hours of "down time" when I was available and not already committed to anything else. Those 15 hours turned into Beers for Gears time.

So the calendar got set up. Two hours every weeknight, a few hours in the morning and again in the evening on the weekends and a few hours in the morning during the week – but *only* when I wasn't committed to doing something else (like traveling/speaking for work or attending a baseball game or a dance recital or having a date night with my wife). And *only* when I wanted to be offering my services.

Six weeks later, my wife asked me if I had made any money at this business yet. "A couple hundred bucks," I said, "Nothing major." She replied, "Good! Go buy a refrigerator because we have no room for food in our fridge; it's full of beer!" Fast-forward to today and suffice it to say, we always have a stack of cash laying around to pay the babysitter and the "direct deposit fridge" (as it's been lovingly renamed) is always full. My neighbors now appreciate "Inventory Reduction Night" as much as they appreciate having a place to bring their bikes for service.

But let's not get caught up in the money and the booze. The real win here is that the only reason this business exists in the first place is because I figured out how to master my calendar and my down time. I never would have been able to do that had I not been committed to putting the Two-Hour Solution into practice consistently, week in and week out.

Putting It All Together Professionally

Back to Aubrey – let's talk about how she put this all together . . .

First, Aubrey recommitted herself to her goals. It really came down to two things: an income goal and a debt-reduction goal (which are kind of tied together, if you think about it). Right off the bat, I noticed a disconnect between where she felt like she wanted to spend her time versus where she actually needed to spend her time, but I waited to see if she noticed it too. She didn't until about three weeks later, when she came to our phone meeting in equal parts exasperation and enlightenment.

"Robb, I have been trying so hard to spend an hour a day going through these files, but I think it might not be the best use of my time."

"Why not?"

"Well, because while it is important to go through these files to find the opportunities, I just feel like I'm spending *all* my best time and energy on this Red Time stuff that is not helping put money in my pocket when I am done. And I am giving up valuable time when my clients are available to meet in the mornings. I keep saying no to morning meetings. I could be meeting with clients, but I'm not because I want to get this done."

Boom-sauce. She figured it out.

From there, we became truly clear on how much she was worth when she was doing her Green Time activities. Hint: It was exponentially more than her Red Time activities. We then discussed how much time she was willing to spend doing those Red Time activities and making sure she wasn't eroding her Green Time. The answer? One hour per week. And you know how she got it done? She came in early four days a week and spent 15 minutes before things got hectic. As you can imagine, it's a bit unmotivating to see a big red chunk of time on your calendar before your day even starts. It's a lot easier to get excited when you know you need to spend only 15 minutes on "grind" work before you get to go make money.

Ready for the fun part? By literally slowing down her approach to combing those files for cross-sales (15 minutes of dedicated effort instead of banging out an hour's worth of shuffling), Aubrey was able to prioritize her most profitable opportunities. Note that she did not abandon the project. She shifted her priorities and set clear intentions for what she wanted to accomplish in those dedicated time slots. She factored in what kind of outreach and follow-up needed to happen in order to close sales with those prospects. And then she made herself available early in the day, when she had the right energy and mindset to ensure a productive meeting.

We continued honing in on her Two-Hour Solution for months. While it was tedious, it definitely paid off. By the end of the year, Aubrey had the following accomplishments under her belt:

- Broke a personal income record.
- Hit an income goal that was *well* above anything she had ever done.
- Paid off her mortgage.
- Wrote more business in one dedicated six-week timeframe than her peers would write all year.
- Took a two-week vacation around the holidays for the first time in six years.
- Stepped into the sensei role at her gym.
- Created three new pieces of art that she was able to sell online.

Not too shabby for one woman in one year.

Advanced Two-Hour Solution Tips

Having clarity on where you are spending your best time and effort is key to making the Two-Hour Solution work for you. Here are a few more tips for maximizing the Two-Hour Solution:

- *Be selfish*: Isolate yourself from colleagues, clients, family members, and distractions. Shut your phone off and get dedicated to *you*. Remember, you need to help yourself before you can help others. Get that "oxygen mask" on good and tight!
- *Reconnect, don't read*: When you are reviewing what's most important to you, it can be easy to just go through the motions of reading what you have written. Be sure you are taking adequate time to reconnect with those important items instead. Remember how excited you were when you crafted your list. Visualize yourself actually living your ideal life,

working your dream job, driving your dream car, and hanging out in your dream home with all your closest friends.

- *Be willing to suck*: I believe it was Brian Tracy who said "Anything worth doing is worth doing poorly at first." For every one of our clients, the Two-Hour Solution is worth doing. But doing it well is a skill. Just like riding a bike or swinging a golf club, the only way to get better at it is to *practice*. One of the most important parts of incorporating the Two-Hour Solution into your life is noticing/realizing what *doesn't* work for you. Too often, we get stuck in a rut, thanks to our habits. The Two-Hour Solution puts those habits on paper right in front of you so that you can see what is and isn't working in your life. Aubrey realized that trying to spend an hour a day on identifying cross sales was eating too much into her day, but without going through the exercise of trying to execute a poorly laid-out plan, she never would have figured out what would work with her calendar.
- *Remember it's a living document*: There's this lovely thing called "Life" that can royally screw up any plan. While you may have a well-defined plan of attack for your week, it's not uncommon for a wrench to make its way into the works, thereby letting the proverbial you-know-what hit the fan. Pay attention to where you can move things around on your calendar so you can address any priorities that need to be addressed, yet still get the things done that you want and need to get done.
- *Be kind to yourself*: If things slip by for 10–20 minutes, just be okay with it. Don't let it become a habit, but at the same time there is no need to rake yourself over the coals if a Green Time call goes long and eats into some red time.
- *Schedule small blocks*: Research says that 90 minutes is about the longest your brain can stay actively engaged/interested in a project before it starts to wander. Use this to your advantage and carve out 90-minute blocks for your Green Time, Red Time, and Flex Time.

- *Guard your Green Time from your Red Time*: Your brain can't distinguish activity from productivity. So many times it gets easy to get into the weeds on a Red Time project when you should be working on Green Time stuff because your activity makes you falsely feel productive. Do you have remedial administrative tasks that need to be accomplished? Hire someone you can trust to make $27 decisions so you can focus on $1,600-an-hour work.
- *Know when you are at your best*: For most folks we talk to, they experience their best energy in the morning. That means clients/prospects/patients probably are at their best in the morning, too. If that's the case for you, try and schedule as much Green Time as you can in the mornings. After all, the biggest checks always get written before 10 a.m. (thanks, Jules!).

  From Robb: I had a client who always caught a second wind at 3:30 in the afternoon. Guess where her calendar showed a big green chunk in her day? That's right . . . 3:30–5:00 p.m., every single day (unless she had a commitment).
- *Utilize immersion*: This normally gets discussed in the "goal setting" conversation, but remember to incorporate your goals into as many aspects of your life as possible. A great way to make sure you do this is by including it in your Two-Hour Solution. Let's say you have a sales goal tied to the number 40. Read for 40 minutes. Carve out a 40-minute workout. Inside that workout, do 40 pushups. Or 40 sit-ups. Or run 4.0 mph on the treadmill (technically just a brisk walk!). Or do 40 Yoga poses that get held for 40 seconds each. Drink 40 ounces of water afterwards. Do another 40 minutes of meditation four times a week. Commit to making 40 calls, or replying to 40 emails. You get the idea.
- *DB6 (Daily Big Six) your time blocks*: It's one thing to have time carved out to get stuff done, but what exactly are you trying to get done in those time blocks? Make a list of the four to six most important things you want or need to accomplish and then work on those things in the order of priority/importance. Start on number one and do not

work on number two until number one is accomplished. Once number one is done, then you can work on number two, but do not begin number three until number two is done, and so on. I didn't create this concept, and it's been described and explained for decades. For a more detailed explanation of the Daily Big Six, including the $450,000 value that was placed on it: google "Charles Schwab Ivy Lee Daily Big Six."

Perfect the Process

This process and the "bonus tips" has been the number-one tool our clients use to harness the "Runaway Brain" we keep referencing. But remember, it all starts with having a clear goal. Without that, it's easy to let you brain "run wild" in an effort to get nowhere in particular. Use this process to avoid the Cheshire Cat scenario. By following this proven process and taking into consideration the nine tips offered above, in a matter of weeks you can start running your life instead of having your life running you.

Chapter Review

- Understand the difference between busy and productive.
- Use the tool to move you from reactive to proactive.
- Value your time (way more than you currently do).
- Know where you want to go before you start moving.

10

Master Your Mind by Mastering the Art of No

Good is the enemy of great.

—Jim Collins, author of Good to Great

Take your greatest weakness . . . and skip it.

—Dan Burrus, global futurist, author, and speaker

The greatest waste of time is doing perfectly that which doesn't need to be done at all.

—Roger Seip, super genius extraordinaire

We've been programmed for *yes*. From a very young age, we're encouraged, raised, cajoled, and sometimes even manipulated to say yes.

"Yes, teacher, I'll do that math problem on the board."

"Yes, Dad, I'll take out the trash."

"Yes, Boss, I'll complete that project."

" Yes, dear, I'll drive the kids to school."

Throughout our lives, we get a lot of rewards, support, and affirmation for saying *yes*. When we enthusiastically say yes, we get smiles, raises, awards, and affection . . . which is 100 percent as it should be.

Don't get us wrong, we adore yes. Heck, we've built our business on yes. Fundamentally, yes is awesome! Yes is the most satisfying word to express, and we want you to be able to have total freedom to say yes to everything in life that you really want to say yes to.

But when in comes to mastering your mind, then too ***much yes can kill you***.

Too much yes can sap your energy, bewilder you, and leave you feeling like you're setting yourself on fire daily, just so that other people can warm up a little. *If you're gonna say yes to the very best, your brain's going to need to say no to everything else. You will have one or the other, but not both.* There's just not enough time for both. So choose.

Case Study: The King of Yes Steps Down from His Throne . . . and Wins!

Like so many of us, when Travis Risvold came to us for coaching he was one of the world's leading experts in yes. As a financial advisor with one of the best companies in the world, he categorically said yes all the time. Every incentive trip, every prospect small or large who wanted to meet, every committee, every service request, every regional meeting of his peers, every everything from everybody, he said yes.

And the result was actually pretty good. Seven years into building his insurance and investment practice, his clients loved him. He was making more money than 90 percent of the people in his hometown, he was winning awards like the "4 Under 40" in his home state. He was recognized as a leader in his church and his local Chamber of Commerce. He was very popular, because if you needed something done and you asked Travis, he would definitely say yes!

The problem was that he said yes to everything, without filtering at all. When we started working with Travis, he said yes so much that he'd lost the ability to say no, and it was really starting to take a toll. The side effects of all this yes were counterproductive, to say the least.

- He was working 70 hours a week in his business.
- He was spending another 10–20 hours a week on church and community obligations.
- Health was becoming a problem—specifically, he was exhausted, gaining weight, and his blood pressure was rising dramatically.
- He was starting to resent everyone.
- Because he said yes to every client all the time, he was overrun with prospects who required a huge amount of energy for very little return.
- When a great prospect (in this case, higher-net-worth individuals) did come along, he was so scattered that he'd often whiff on those opportunities due to lack of preparation.

Yes had gotten him to a real breaking point, and it wasn't going to get any better, unless he started saying no. It was absolutely vital that he start saying no to good/mediocre stuff, so that he could say yes to the really great stuff. We know, that all sounds well and good, but it's easier said than done.

Nobody Likes No

The thing is, no pretty much sucks—it just doesn't feel good. We don't like hearing no, and we don't like saying it either. We carry a lot of wiring in our brains that makes no really scary.

Back in the days when we needed a tribe to survive, the absolute worst thing that could happen to you was to get kicked out of your tribe. If you were left alone without a family or clan to protect you, it was a death sentence.

The fastest way to get kicked out of your tribe would be to have a disagreement with the leader, or to be perceived as not making a contribution. Social interactions and pleasing people (especially authority figures) became supremely important, so over millennia of genetics and thousands of generations of upbringing, we've had a deep-seated fear of displeasing others hardwired into our genetics.

Back in the day, rejection actually meant death. Clearly that's not the case anymore, but rejection is still incredibly scary. And when you say no, you run the risk of rejection. So we resist it to our detriment.

The T Ris Protocol

Travis has this yes tendency even more than most, so we immediately implemented a couple of strategies:

- We had to lay a foundation that would actually make no a more pleasant option than yes, and simultaneously make it more acceptable to those he needed to say no to.
- We needed to identify just a few specific things to say no to. You can't just start categorically telling everyone to screw off, right? We had to pick his battles.

We realized that our solutions were actually universal, so we're including the T Ris Protocol here. The foundation piece integrated a lot of the basics that we've covered in *Master Your Mind*:

- Clarity about his core values and overall vision for his business gave Travis a strong internal compass, plus enough sense of purpose that he simply cared less what people thought.
- That clarity, combined with a regular practice of the Two-Hour Solution gave him enough of a plan and enough forward momentum that people didn't want to get in his way (in a healthy, respectful way, not in a bossy, scary way)
- Systematically upgrading his self-talk turned on his "money magnet," so that higher-quality clients and prospects

started wanting to get on his calendar *first.* This naturally left less space for the time-wasters or "lower-grade" clients.

This foundation supported Travis so that he was always in a position of strength, as opposed to desperation. For you sales professionals, you can imagine that on its own, this total lack of desperation boosted his sales results (remember "the power of not caring"?). And then once Travis started strategically saying no, well – let's just say it got really fun for him.

- He freed up massive quantities of positive energy.
- He's almost completely removed feelings of guilt and shame.
- His "per hour" rate of revenue generation more than doubled, overnight.
- He's making significantly more money and accomplishing goals that were previously thought impossible, while working about 60 percent of the hours he used to.
- All of which is really nice, considering that he loves spending time with his beautiful wife and newborn son.

Here's what Travis mastered his mind to say no to, which you might want to consider emulating.

Say No to Certain People

It is impossible to say yes to everyone. We'd like it to be different, but it's not. We're wired to think that we have the biggest impact when we say yes to the largest number of people, but that's simply not how life works.

We have the biggest impact when we say yes to the largest number of the right people, whom we can actually help, and we're coming from a place where we're equipped to help them. The *quality* of your yesses is at least as important as the *quantity.* When you try to say yes to everyone, you end up doing a disservice to everyone . . . especially the ones you care about the most. This is where yes really backfires.

Travis identified three groups of people he had to let go of, two in his business and one in his life.

Saying No to Business Group #1: Travis's "B" and "C" Clients

In a business like Travis's, the practice of segmenting your client base into different strata is really common, and becomes absolutely necessary once a book of business gains any size at all. Teaching Sales Professionals how to do this is the subject of numerous books and coaching programs in any given industry, so we won't do an extensive dissertation. Let's just work on the mentality that's necessary, and remove some guilt from the process.

Assigning grades like A, B, C, and D sounds so judgmental that we feel bad doing it, just like assigning levels like silver, gold, platinum, and diamond. Whatever grading scale you use, it's easy to feel like you're judging someone's worth as a person. Please understand that's not what you're doing. You're not grading the client, *you're grading your ability to impact them*, and in return their ability to impact you or your business.

Travis's segmented groups were pretty easy to identify just by looking at his calendar. Once the B and C clients were identified, the action step was really simple . . . *just stop going after them so vigorously*. Travis needed to embrace the fact that he was no longer a rookie.

In the first five years of building his practice, Travis made the totally appropriate commitment to go hard after every single opportunity. And for the first five years this was the right way to do it – in almost any business there's a ramp-up period where the answer actually is to just put the pedal to the metal.

But six years in, the 80/20 rule had really started rearing its head. It was glaringly obvious that 20 percent of his client base was indeed producing 80 percent of his revenue. That 20 percent – that group of A clients – *adored* Travis, was the source of very few headaches, and truly derived the greatest value from the relationship. The other 80 percent loved to talk to him, and so would unconsciously invent questions and scenarios . . . but only when he called them. So he decided to let go of them just a little. Instead of calling every 12 weeks just to "see what's up and if he can help," he's now calling these folks every 6–12 months. Just this change has freed up 5–10 hours every single week.

Saying No to Business Group #2: Figments of the Imagination

The other shockingly large group of people that Travis was pouring *rivers* of energy into were figments of his imagination. Every day (literally every single day), there were two to six calls scheduled on his calendar with people he felt obligated to reach out to because they were clients of his company at some point in the past 10 years. Now these calls had never been productive—more than 90 percent of the time they never answered the phone, and when they did, the results were always mediocre at best. Key to understand . . . these folks were not expecting his call and genuinely didn't care. In many cases they likely wouldn't even recognize Travis's name.

These calls had been so unproductive for so long that Travis had started dreading them. Every time he saw one on the calendar his brain would immediately start resisting, and the result was that he would reschedule the date of the call for eight weeks later. You can imagine what happened as the effects of this practice piled up. Every week he was faced with a growing list of people whom he knew would be a waste of time, but he felt obligated to call anyway . . . but he'd made the whole story up in his head. The "need" to make these calls was a figment of his imagination. So we asked him to stop going after these entirely. Not just less vigorously—entirely.

The mechanism we used still cracks us up: Instead of rescheduling these calls for eight weeks later, we asked Travis to reschedule them for 100 years later. So Travis doesn't feel like he's jettisoning these lovely folks entirely, he'll "just get to it in 100 years." His calendar in the year 2119 is chockful of calls, but it's not really stressing him out much anymore. This was another change that has freed up 5–10 hours a week for Travis, and an amount of energy that is nearly impossible to even measure. He no longer feels apprehension or dread when looking at his call list for the week, only enthusiasm, gratitude, and world-class motivation.

Saying No to People Who Simply Suck: Energy Vampires and Flat-Out Jerks

The third group of people Travis needed to say no to (and likely you need to, too?) were the small group of people in his universe who simply suck. When we say "suck," we mean it in both the slang sense and the literal. There are people who literally just suck the energy out of you, usually through a tendency to gossip and/or dwell on negativity. These are the folks who brighten the room . . . when they leave. You're probably not one of these, unless you are – in which case we're really glad you're reading this.

As an input source, the people you spend time with are massively influential. If you have kids, you know you're aggressively watching who your kids are hanging out with, right? That's because you know that *your* kids will become like *those* kids, whether they want to or not. That doesn't stop once you reach adulthood. Brian Tracy taught us that "the selection of the wrong peer group can ruin a career all by itself." You've got to be aggressive in monitoring this input source, and therefore pretty ruthless in saying no to people who simply suck.

Being the people pleaser that he is, Travis had to reconcile it this way:

> I'm not actually saying *no* to them per se. I'm saying *no* to gossip, drama, and negativity. If they were carrying measles, I would stay away from them, aggressively keep my family away from them, and feel zero guilt about it. Gossip, drama, and negativity are *much* worse for me than chicken pox, they're just somehow more socially acceptable. When I look at it this way, it becomes really easy to avoid the energy drain that comes from people who just suck.

Revisiting "Be Too ___"

Certainly the most elegant way to say no to this group is to proactively replace it with people and projects that fill you up and move you forward. Be too busy having lunch with someone uplifting to meet up for coffee and negativity. Sometimes mastering your mind involves just crowding out negative thoughts with a huge volume of positive ones, and who you spend time with is no different.

Travis Risvold now has a calendar that's so full of people who are awesome for him that there's just no room for suckers . . . and if one of them does happen to get through, he's got such a deep reservoir of energy and patience that the effects just bounce right off. Yet another upgrade that is difficult to overstate.

Say No to Certain Activities

"Maybe even more important than the *to-do* list is the *stop doing* list."

—*Jim Collins and many others*

In addition to saying *no* to certain *individuals*, there are almost certainly some *things you're doing* where you'd benefit from either outsourcing or flat-out skipping – put your learning hat on, because you're about to learn how to not just master your mind, but exponentially multiply your time.

Math That Motivates

Just now we brought up the 80/20 principle, as it applied to people. Same principle applies to your activities or your time:

Twenty percent of your activities generate 80 percent of your results.

Twenty percent of your time makes you 80 percent of your income.

Let's do some math that we've done with our clients. Word problems – yay!

If Johnny makes $100,000 a year and works 50 hours a week with two weeks' vacation, how much does Johnny make per hour?

Well this seems pretty easy – he works 50 hours a week for 50 weeks a year, so that's 2,500 hours. Divide $100,000 by 2,500 hours and you see that Johnny makes $40 per hour. Right?

Not when you understand that the 80/20 rule applies to time. The reality here is that Johnny has some time where he gets paid like a celebrity doctor, and a lot where he gets paid like a teenager at a fast-food restaurant . . . and so do you.

If 20 percent of Johnny's time in this equation nets 80 percent of his income, that means only 500 of his yearly hours nets $80,000 of his income. That's $160 an hour.

Then the other 2,000 hours of his year earns him $20,000. The math is easy . . . It's $10 per hour, which is less than minimum wage in a lot of places.

When Travis realized that this was almost his exact situation, he almost vomited.

We can pretty well guarantee you've got a similar dynamic – we've picked up a situation like this with 100 percent of our clients so far, so the likelihood is high. And if your income is higher than Johnny's (or if you're moving in that direction), the nausea only becomes greater as you realize you've been saying yes to a lot of minimum wage activities and therefore been unavailable for the truly rewarding opportunities.

Our clients experience that the fastest benefit from mastering their minds is when they start saying no to the 80 percent of time and activities that returns next to nothing. Saying no here can go two ways: You can take an activity and *outsource it*, or you can just *skip it*.

Outsource It: For Goodness Sake, Just Pay Someone!

Some of the activities that you can say no to are just classic "Red Time" activities. Paperwork, organization, basic logistics – these are things that need to be done, but they just don't require a lot of brainpower or focus.

This type of activity is crying out for you to hire it done. Paying $20/hour for work that you get paid $10/hour for may seem like a ripoff . . . until you realize that you can now make

$160 with that hour! Volumes have been written about how to outsource and/or delegate, so we'll not go into deep detail here. One of the bigger influences on us in this regard is Timothy Ferriss's classic *The 4-Hour Workweek*—read it and thank us later.

What we will encourage you to do is to please let go of the idea that you can do *everything* better than anyone else can. This is a common story that achievers tell themselves and get trapped by. Just get over this fallacy . . . It's probably not true, and even if it is true, it's irrelevant. There are only so many hours in the day, and we have to choose how we spend them. Choose wisely and let your team or your systems take care of them for you. A small investment of money and a little "letting go" will serve you well.

Just Skip It

And then there are the things that you can just . . . let go. We know—we can hear the voice in your head right now:

> Really? Are you saying that there are things I should just not do at all . . . like *never again*?!

Bingo.

It's likely not a lot of things, but if one of us were working with you in coaching, it wouldn't take long to identify a small handful of activities you should just drop. Remember Travis and the calls that we rescheduled for a 100 years down the road? We actually suggested scheduling them for 100 years in the past—the whole point was that he was never to do that activity again.

One of the biggest places where we just hemorrhage time, energy, and money is when we try to do perfectly the thing that just doesn't need to be done at all. A mundane but relevant example from Roger's life follows.

Case Study: Just Skip It

Forever, we've been Christmas card people. Like all of our friends, we'd send Christmas Cards with the family pictures out to hundreds of people, every year . . . until last year. Between a period of intense activity in both of our businesses synchronized with some health crises on both sides of our family, we just never got around to it.

Around December 10, there was actually a moment where my wife (who, if we're being honest, was the one who did all the Christmas card work) looked at me and said, "I think this year's cards just ain't happening," and I agreed we should be okay with that. So none of our friends got Christmas cards from the Seips in 2017. And you know what?

Nobody noticed.

It's not just that we got no negative feedback; we got no feedback of any kind. For our friends, the lack of a Seip Christmas card literally didn't register at all. On anyone. Don't get me wrong, we love Christmas and we love our friends, but it became pretty clear that the hours and dollars that we'd invested every year in getting that done were in many ways totally unnecessary. When we skipped it, there was zero effect."

In your business and your life, we'd bet there's something like the Christmas card drought for you . . . maybe several. Do yourself a favor—take some things that seem necessary and consider the following questions:

- "Is this need I'm feeling perhaps just a story I'm telling myself?"
- "What would really happen if I just skipped this?"

We'd actually encourage you to experiment with "skipping it" in lots of areas, but start with this one.

You know how you respond to every email or text immediately? Try skipping that and see how much that small "no" improves your sanity and productivity. It's a small step, but one that can lead to a lot of really nice places.

Yes is wonderful, Yes is beautiful, and mastering your mind requires that you use your *no*.

Chapter Review

- Yes is maybe the best word in the language, but too much yes can kill you.
- We're wired for yes, so mastering your mind requires working at saying no.
- You likely need to say no to certain people—perhaps "lower-grade" folks in your business, definitely the figments of your imagination, and definitely those who just suck.
- You almost certainly need to say no to some activities—observe the shocking math of the 80/20 rule and either outsource that activity or simply skip it.

11

Master Your Mind by Mastering Your Environment: Declutter

There's no such thing as multitasking, there's just a willingness to suck at more than one thing at the same time.

—*Robb Zbierski, un-sucker of things*

Likely the most intuitive of the "counterintuitive" strategies we are sharing, the idea of decluttering is essential to mastering your mind. After all, what's easier to manage, a handful of things or dozens of things all at the same time?

It's funny, when we were out doing the market research for this book, whenever the topic of "decluttering" came up as a theme of the book, that was the one phrase that always got an "Oh, *gosh*, do I need that!" Or "*Man*, do my direct reports need to learn about *that*!" from whomever we were talking with.

So it begs the question, why do we constantly need a reminder to get rid of what we don't need? If it isn't essential to our success/progress/livelihood, why do we insist on hoarding everything we can until it totally consumes us? I think it has to do with that whole caveman mentality we discussed in Chapter 1. Caveman mentality ("What's coming to get me? How do I fight it off?") plus YOLO (you only live once) plus FOMO (fear of missing out) leads us to grab everything we can and hold onto it "just in case." And in our rapid-pace world, we grab on to every little bite-sized thing we can. Tweets, articles, updates, tips, tricks, books, pamphlets, thoughts, quotes, ideas . . . you get the picture. And then without a proper clearing out, they add up and add up until you literally can't see success because it is blocked by the pile of junk sitting between where you are and where you want to be.

When it comes to decluttering, there are two main areas you can focus on:

1. Physical decluttering
2. Mental decluttering

Let's take a look at each one of these individually, and then talk about how they are actually one and the same.

Physical Decluttering

We talked earlier about the idea of slowing down in order to accelerate your results. Sometimes slowing down means removing things from the equation. It means thinning the herd or trimming the fat or culling the weeds. Want to get better results? Make life a zero-sum game. Eliminate anything that won't guarantee you a "win." Here's an example from Robb.

Case Study: Decluttering

When my wife and I bought our home in Illinois, we learned firsthand the importance of decluttering in order to move forward. And it came from an unlikely place . . .

We had invited our families over to help celebrate the new place (and help us with some work that needed to happen before moving in). As we were bringing the food out to the back deck, we picked up on a pungent odor. Skunk. The house backed up to a busy road, so I assumed that one had been hit by a car. I was wrong. After a few minutes, we realized the odor was coming from right beneath us, under the deck. Dinner was quickly moved inside and we tested out the A/C as the windows had to be closed up.

Over the next few weeks, we kept picking up on the scent, but in weird places all over the outside of the house and the yard. And it was severely limiting the number of places we felt we could be in the yard, especially with three-year-old twins.

After watching a skunk run across our deck one night, my wife and I decided to start narrowing down the list of places they could be. We got it down to two: under the deck and in the forsythia bushes on the side of our house.

We decided to make it a zero-sum game for the skunk and since it's a lot easier to cut down bushes than a deck, we started with the forsythia. As anyone who has bought a home knows, there is always a *long* "Honey-do" list for the first year. We had spent one of our first weekends clearing out the dead branches in another set of bushes earlier in the summer, so I had a pretty good idea of what we were in for.

As I was cutting the bushes down, it started looking a bit scary. The growth was so overgrown and tangled that it became obvious the only way to manage the bushes was a full-on hacking.

We were a bit nervous about what a barren side of the house was going to look like until I glanced back and saw the other bushes we had cleaned out earlier in the year. They were flourishing. Any person with a green thumb will tell you that in order to make sure your plants grow, you need to clear our the dead stuff. If not, it will just choke out the good stuff and you'll be left with mediocre landscaping.

So out went the bushes. And you know what? We found out the skunk was under the deck. Talk about a punch in the gut! But I knew there was a lesson there, and here it is.

Eliminating old growth leads creates new opportunity.

Because we figured out where the skunk wasn't, it allowed us to repurpose that spot into a lovely garden. And the deck *definitely* got torn down.

Let's be honest though. Skunks and gardens and decks and patios aren't going to help you be more successful. Let's look at a couple of other scenarios where physically decluttering led to positive change.

Piles of Business under Piles of Paperwork

Mary is a top-producing realtor in her company. She has represented the industry at the local level and the statewide level, gaining critical acclaim for her ability to lead while still maintaining her top producer status within her company.

Mary has a *ton* going on, and as a result, her desk often gets messy. Not because she is sloppy, but just as a byproduct of the sheer amount of activity she is engaging in on a daily basis. About once a month, she simply needs to spend time to reorganize it before things get unruly. However, Mary *really* likes to clean her desk whenever she sees a lull in her business.

In her words, "I don't know what it is, but whenever I am looking for that one piece of business, I need to hit a goal or break a record or turn the tide, I *always* find it after a thorough desk cleaning. Sometimes it's a lost prospect that gets uncovered, and sometimes it's just the fact that I have more mental availability as I'm not thinking about sorting through my mess. But regardless of the scenario, I *do* know that every time I take the time to thoroughly clean and organize my workspace, I always find at least a couple of thousand dollars in commissions that I didn't have before I started!"

Now please don't be mistaken – there are not literal piles of money lying underneath her paperwork. But the money shows up in people calling her out of the blue or her following up with someone and finally getting a "yes."

Understand what is happening here. By literally removing clutter and distraction and "mess" from her situation, Mary is uncovering opportunities to make money and continue to grow her business.

Roger does the same thing, only with his car. (Full disclosure: I am *not* asking permission to share this, which means I'll likely need to ask Roger for forgiveness when the book comes out!)

Roger spends a *lot* of time in his car. Sometimes I don't know how he does it. I'm talking four-hour, six-hour, sometimes even eight-hour one-way trips to travel and speak for clients. When home, he's often shuttling one or both of the boys to or from school or sports or the beach or a friend's house. As you can imagine, a good amount of fast-food wrappers, toll-booth receipts, gas receipts, books, handouts, sporting equipment, coffee mugs, and clothes tend to accumulate in the car. I'm not telling you this to paint an ugly, cluttered picture of Roger. I'm telling you this because of what he shared with me a few years ago when he got a new car.

When he got the new car, he made it a personal mission to keep it as clean as possible. That meant weekly trips to the car wash to keep it looking tidy, both inside and out. A byproduct of this new habit has been a consistent run of results that keep shattering a personal sales and revenue record for him month after month (after 20-plus years of experience).

It's kind of like when you are trying to figure out a food allergy. The first thing the doctor or nutritionist will do is strip everything out of your diet to the point where you're eating virtually nothing. After that, they slowly introduce one new type of food at a time until you know your body can handle it. Only after proving that your body is not allergic to that food will you add another food to the mix. Similarly, in your brain, sometimes you just need to strip everything out and start from scratch. Having all that mental availability often leads you to have new thought processes that are better, clearer, faster and more effective than ways you have thought in the past. Here's an example.

I met George years ago at a Memory Training workshop, and we had kept in touch as he often had questions due to being a meticulous student. He reached out to me when changing companies as he was kind of stuck and needed a coach to get him past the threshold where he had gotten on his own. (Sound familiar? A common denominator of successful people is that they seek for help, especially when looking to create a mental and results breakthrough.)

As part of the discovery process I came to find out that George kept every single article he ever read that was written by every coach or guru or self-help professional he heard of, *ever*. After some candid question and answer sessions, George finally decided to share with me that he was a self-proclaimed "personal development alcoholic" (this has since become one of my favorite lines). Over the years, he had managed to amass somewhere between six and eight bankers boxes full of articles printed off the Internet, magazine articles that had been clipped out, newspaper articles and industry journals that he had collected. This collection had taken over his dining room. His wife, in particular, was not a fan of the fact that this collection had also taken over their ability to host dinner parties, as the dining room looked more like a cross between a library and an episode of *Hoarders*.

The funny thing was that, according to George, he never went back to read the articles that he saved. He saw something that he thought would be useful, and stuck it in one of the bankers boxes with the idea that "I'll probably get back to it down the road." Needless to say, "down the road" never happened, and George's clutter was the leading cause of frustration at home, frustration at work, and frustration in his marriage. I'm sure you can imagine what happened next.

Over the course of a couple of painful weeks for George, he figured out what he needed and what was just taking up space. The end result was that he recycled over 80 percent of what he thought he needed in those resources. We literally helped him physically declutter his dining room. The great news is that George and his wife were able to host a dinner party for the first time in three years. Also, George's results started to improve, as he had less mental anguish over what he wasn't reading and more mental availability to focus on servicing his clients. Not long after the purge, he was recognized as the number-two producing agent within his firm.

Does this sound like something that would benefit you? Next is the process that George and I went through to get his dining room back to a dining room, and his results back to where he wanted them to be.

A Quick Way to Slow by 70 Percent

One of the best ways to clear your mind is some form of exercise, but reading is also another great area where you can clear out overgrowth. It's great to let some new opinions and ideas come in and either supplement or replace old thoughts, beliefs, and habits that you have formed.

I know, "read more" gets shoved down your throat time after time, Heck, you are reading a book right now! But a lot of times, the desire to read and learn can get "overgrown" with the list of stuff you "should" be reading.

Do you have the "I'll get to it" pile? You know the one I'm talking about. It usually sits either behind you or just out of your peripheral vision. It's the months' worth of trade journals or newsletters or books you bought at a conference that you haven't even opened yet. It sits behind you or just out of your peripheral vision so that you don't stress yourself out about not reading it. Every time you see it, you start "shoulding" all over yourself, which in turn speeds up the mind and the excuses and increases the stress. Let's nip this in the bud, shall we?

Here's a process we share with clients that typically results in at *least* a 70 percent reduction in their reading workload:

Step 1: Gather *all* the materials you have accumulated and gather them into one pile.

Step 2: Rank each piece on a scale of 1–10 relative to its importance to you achieving your goal(s). If a piece is absolutely crucial to your success, it's a 10. If it has nothing to do with your job or your life, or it's been sitting in the pile for over a year, it's a 1. Place each piece in its own pile with other pieces of the same ranking (hint: you'll end up with 10 piles).

Step 3: Take everything rated 6 or lower and *throw it away*! (or consult your local trash collection provider for recycling options).

Step 4: Through your Two-Hour Solution (see Chapter 9), read your "7 and above" materials during your Excellence Time.

Step 5: Enjoy the extra time, knowledge, and experience that comes with spending the right amount of time reading the right kinds of information that keeps you on track with what you want to achieve.

What's the Alternative?

"So what?" you may ask. "I've been running it hot all my life and I've done okay!" All well and good, but what you might not realize is that running it hot can lead to misfires. And those misfires, added up over time, can lead to a Runaway Brain.

Mental Decluttering

This chapter has been full of stories about skunks and bankers boxes and messy cars and messy desks. How is this going to help you? It's a proxy you can follow in getting a mental clearing to take place. Oftentimes, we find ourselves "overgrown" or "stacked up" in life, in relationships, in money, or in projects. We get there because we just "let it be" without actually doing anything, right or wrong.

By nature, your brain will run its course and build up lots of unhealthy ideas. And some of those ideas really stink! Just like the farmer who has to methodically manage weeds in his field, you have to manage your thoughts and beliefs and inputs and surroundings. The best way to do that is to clear out the old growth. And then, sometimes, you gotta just slash and burn.

Habits often get discussed in a very positive light, but more often than not they cause more problems than they do progress. Taking the time to do a mental audit on the habits you have formed over time can be one of the most beneficial ways to declutter mentally.

Make New Mental Habits

Do you travel? If so, what do you read or watch or listen to when you are on the plane/train/car? Instead of grabbing the latest issue of *People* magazine, try a copy of *Wired* or *Inc.* instead, to keep you abreast of new technology and trends. While the list of available movies is always nice, try a documentary on Netflix or Amazon Prime that might help expand your knowledge base and help you engage in more thoughtful conversation with your friends and peers.

There's a whole chapter on how to start your day, but when is the last time you really evaluated what you were doing and when you were doing it in your day? What new affirmations or thoughts can you use to "feed your Elephant" to make sure that your day is optimized from the first minute.

Ask more and better questions. One of the biggest things I see people do when faced with adversity is to just kind of take it for what it is, instead of questioning what could be different. Any time you experience a failure or a miss or a loss, ask how that outcome could potentially be the best result possible. Over time, this shift in perspective will lend itself well to dealing with any major disruptions that come up in life. One of the best pieces of advice we ever heard with regard to increasing success was to "Keep your highs low and your lows high." The more work you do to maintain an even keel, the easier the rest of your life becomes. As the old French saying goes, "When the training is hard, the battle is easy."

When it's all said and done, there are a multitude of things you can do to get decluttered in your life both physically and mentally. Taking time to do this periodically will help you get rid of obstacles, messes, disruptions, confusion, and failure. This newfound clarity, both physically and mentally, will allow you to expand your thinking and your mindset, leading to better results, faster results, and more opportunity for goodness to enter your life.

Chapter Review

- Two types of decluttering are beneficial: mental and physical.
- Removing what is unnecessary from your environment will allow you to focus on and maximize the necessary.
- Old habits die hard. Try something new.
- Reading is a great way to get out of a mental rut, but pay attention to how much you are adding to your bandwidth.

12

Master Your Mind by Mastering Your Body: Take Care of Yourself

Forget about managing your time . . .
manage your energy instead.

—*Harvard Business Review*

Keep Your Battery Level High

One of the most effective strategies for "slowing down the game" in order to be more successful is mastering the art of taking care of yourself.

The idea of taking care of yourself has been talked about, discussed, written about, and I dare say beaten to death in the past many decades. But this is for a good reason. It works, and it's often one of the simplest things you can focus on in order to create habits that drive positive change.

Anyone with a mobile phone understands that you need to take care of it in order for it to work. Drop it too many times and you literally can't see what's on the screen. At the very least, you need to plug it in so it has enough juice to work. One of Robb's favorite scenarios to play out with groups usually sounds like this:

RZ: How many of you have done the thing where you wake up, look over at your nightstand, and realize you forgot to plug your phone in overnight?

Crowd: Most of the room raises their hand and laughs or mumbles something negative or both.

RZ: Okay, and then what is the first response you have or the first words out of your mouth when you realize you forgot to plug your phone in overnight?"

Crowd: Ninety-five percent of the room said, "Oh, s#!t!" Five percent of the room said, "Oh, fu&#!" (True story, the loudest f-bomb I ever heard was at an HR convention!)

RZ: And why is that your first response? Why do you start your day screaming curse words? It's because you know there is only so far you can get in your day before you have to *stop* being productive and go fix that.

Everyone we talk to agrees that their clients, their family members, their friends, even their colleagues can *all* tell if or when they show up with a half-charged battery. And they all admit that it's difficult to get through the day staying focused on one thing as they keep needing to divert their depleted energy (a.k.a. stop to plug it in) during the course of the day.

You Won't Like Me When I'm Angry

Our friend Bob is a perfect case study. Bob is an elite, internationally recognized, and renowned periodontist. Bob splits his time between two practices that are a 60-minute flight from each other. On his busiest days, he sees as many as 70 patients in a day. Additionally, Bob is the director of two dental study clubs, one in each market he services. When he isn't practicing, Bob is called upon to lecture at other study clubs and dental events throughout the year in order to help other comprehensive dentists and their teams learn how to perform the types of intricate procedures he does at the level that he does.

Bob and Robb were both asked to present at a dental convention. Robb ended up getting there the day before the event started, but Bob got there the morning it started. After a full day of seeing patients, he hopped on a cross-country red-eye flight in order to arrive before the event started. However, Bob didn't come straight to the ballroom when he got to the hotel at 6 a.m. Instead, Bob went to the gym in order to fit in a quick workout. When we asked him why he went to work out after a five-hour red-eye flight, his response was simple yet poignant: "Because if I didn't, I'd be an asshole all day!"

Brash? Yes (but not really, if you know Bob). But read between the lines on this one . . . Bob knew that he was busy. He knew that he had a lot going on and he knew that he needed to be on point in order to bring as much value as he could to the event. If Bob didn't slow down for 30 minutes and focus on doing what he needed to do in order to get in the right state of mind, he was not going to be (a) helpful, or (b) fun to be around.

Needless to say, his strategy (and approach) worked. Bob's presentation was exceptional, and one of the highlights of the entire event. And it was all because of his ability to stop "grinding it out" and take a bit of time to get refocused.

Ways to "Plug In"

What are you doing to keep your proverbial battery at full charge? There's a ton of options.

What does your diet look like? This is not a nutrition book, we are not nutritionists, but what you read earlier about your mental input applies here to your diet: Garbage in equals garbage out.

How often are you taking an hour or a day off? What about a week? Have you scheduled your down time? Are you using the Two-Hour Solution (see Chapter 9) to its full extent? The chief marketing officer of a Fortune 500 company we know stands behind his theory that his success is a direct result of taking at *least* two months off every year. In his words, "I'm almost amazed at how much more focused, energized, and productive I am when I have only 10 months to accomplish what we want to accomplish over the course of 12!"

What does your exercise routine look like? Again, we're not in the business of fitness and nutrition but we know story after story of folks whose lives have been changed just by making the decision to be more active. As of the writing of this book, Robb's grandmother is in the advanced stages of dementia. We watched her mother go through the same thing. It is a long, frustrating process that has no rhyme or reason for good days or bad days. One day she is laughing and hugging everyone, the next day she is convinced that we are trying to steal from her and biting the nurse. It's not the best thing we have ever gone through. While it has been a long road with lots of good days and lots of not-so-good days, without question, some of her best days happen when she gets a chance to get up and walk around for a bit.

If you are reading this book, we're imagining you are the kind of person who loves to help other people. You understand that bringing value to another person's business or life increases the value of yours. But here's the thing to keep in mind. In order for you to provide the best help possible, you need to make sure you are helping yourself first and foremost. Take the time to rest and recharge the battery.

As Mother Theresa said (we paraphrase), "Find the closest person to you and help that person." For so many people we work with, the closest people are *their own selves*! Focusing on others to the point where you are compromising your own happiness, health, energy, or "me time" is of no help in the bigger picture. It's okay to get selfish and take the time you need in order to take care of yourself. But don't get stressed about needing to take an entire day or a week or two months off. Just like the newest phones, even just a quick 15 minutes of down time can get you a couple more hours of "talk time."

Be Kind to Yourself

We discussed mastering your self-talk in an earlier chapter, but this concept applies to mastering how to taking care of yourself. After all, thoughts become feelings. Those feelings create emotions, and emotion is what drives physical action and change.

How you talk to yourself, what you say to yourself, and the words you choose to use have a *massive* impact on your ability to be more successful at every single thing that you do. The thoughts and words you use to describe yourself can often have the biggest impact on your quality of life. Too many people we meet or talk with haven't mastered the often-overlooked skill of simply being kind to themselves.

We apply so much unneeded pressure to ourselves – pressure to support the family or perform at work or to be a great spouse or partner or parent. Pressure to get "likes" and "shares" on social media. Pressure to win. That pressure leads to stress, which leads to deflecting thoughts and feelings into something that is easier to stomach, which is humor. Often that humor can lead to self-deprecation.

"There is a fine line between self-deprecation and self-abuse. How you consistently talk to yourself often determines which side of the line you end up living on." – Robb Z

But this is a slippery slope. After all, since the brain loves negativity, it becomes intrinsically easier to let thoughts, phrases, and feelings default to the negative. And other people can always relate to negativity, so you end up unconsciously beating yourself up for no reason other than to try and relate to people. You end up victimizing yourself!

Stop self-deprecating. At least try to minimize it. It is not serving you and is actually counterproductive. Here's an example. One of the least helpful answers to the questions "How's it going?" is this:

"Better than I deserve!"

On the surface, it seems decent. Kind of funny, pretty vague, maybe suggests some level of gratitude. But here's what your brain hears:

> "I don't deserve success or happiness or cause for celebration. As a matter of fact, I'm lucky to be alive at this point!"

And then that person is always confused why "Things don't go my way" or wonders "Why don't people respect me?"

Simply choosing to hold yourself in high regard and believing that you are "worth it" helps portray an air of confidence. And confidence is what will set you apart. Master this skill of practicing kindness on yourself and it will extend to how kind you are to others. You'll be surprised at how quickly others will flock to you for support, guidance, and input. Because after all . . .

When you are on fire, people will come from miles to watch you burn.

You Look Ma-a-ahvelous!

Another way to take care of yourself is to literally take . . . care . . . of . . . yourself. Physically. Pay attention to how you look and how you dress. Before we go any further, no, we are not going to rehash the scene from *The Devil Wears Prada* where Meryl Streep chastises Anne Hathaway for wearing the cerulean blue sweater. But we do need to talk about how looking good helps you feel good and the impact that has on mastering your mental game.

In his best-selling book *How I Raised Myself from Failure to Success In Selling*, Frank Bettger talked about one of the things he did early on was to schedule himself a haircut every two weeks for the purpose of keeping himself looking prim and proper. By knowing he had a scheduled appointment to maintain his style, he was able to focus his energy into selling. The title of the book alone tells you it worked.

In any beginner sales training course, they always say to dress just a tiny bit better than your customer. One of our friends who used to sell advertising for a major magazine in New York City always insisted on wearing a suit and tie to meetings with bicycle companies (notorious for their casual dress code). When asked why, he simply stated, "I *always* want to be the best-looking guy in the room when I am asking for money!"

Again, there are volumes upon volumes of books and articles on the power of fashion and its role in business. Take for example the coach who changed companies and immediately got a full makeover (hair, makeup, wardrobe) in an effort to make a fresh start with the new organization. She decided it was time for a change and the first thing to change was her appearance. Last we heard she was breaking records with the new company

Probably our favorite example of how your physical appearance impacts your confidence and swagger is from film. Go watch *Trading Places* with Eddie Murphy and Dan Aykroyd. The entire film is all about how success in business can be tied to appearance. It's a classic film that *definitely* earned its R rating.

Movie references aside, is it time to take a personal style inventory and see if you need to make any upgrades to your wardrobe? A few years ago we both invested heavily with our haberdasher. We were starting to get a lot more work with high-level firms and organizations and the department store suits we were showing up in just weren't cutting it.

Is it time for a new haircut?

From Robb: I'll often change my hairstyle throughout the year just to shake it up and depending on how I am feeling. A few examples from just the past 12 moths include long hair, short hair, and a shaved head. I grew a beard one year. That was interesting, but it made for some confusion when I sent a head shot of a burly bearded dude to the Wholesale Lumber Association and then this hairless mouse of a man showed up to speak!

Some of the rest of these may seem petty or superficial, but if these things are on your list of improvements that might make you feel better and more confident, give them a shot!

- Do you need a new hairstyle?
- Need to cover up or remove a tattoo? Need a new tattoo?
- New glasses, or switch to contacts, or Lasik surgery?
- New makeup?

- New wardrobe?
- New suit(s)?
- Do you want to get your teeth straightened or whitened or replaced (implants are awesome!)?
- New car?
- New briefcase or bag?
- New shoes? New laces? Fun socks?

The possibilities are endless in this category, so have some fun. If even one tiny change helps boost your confidence, the entire exercise was worth it (see the 2-millimeter principle in Chapter 5).

Chapter Review

- Taking care of your body helps take care of your thinking.
- Rest or take down time when it is needed.
- Know your limits.
- Be kind to yourself.
- Your physical appearance impacts your mental game.

13

Master Your Mind by Mastering Silence and Presence: Shut Up and Listen

You were blessed with two ears and one mouth. Use them proportionately.

—*Unknown*

You say it best . . . when you say nothing at all.

—*Alison Krauss, Grammy-winning singer/songwriter*

While this is not a "communication skills" book, one of the ways you can truly master your mind is by paying closer attention to your communication skills. By this, I mean pay closer attention to both how you talk to yourself and how you talk to other people. One of the clearest examples we see of people moving too fast and hampering their results is in verbal communication. With the proliferation of texting, email, and social media, it feels like conversations have gotten smaller, shorter, fewer and further between, and, most concerning, totally sound reactive in nature instead of connective. Whereas just a few years ago we had to wait until after 9 p.m. to use our unlimited minutes, nowadays, we leave hours on the table because we try to communicate with the least number of characters possible. However, where you think that a quick message can get the job done *now*, it's often counterproductive, leading to a whole string of messages that aren't even close to the topic you started discussing. "In the weeds" is where a lot of miscommunication, speculation, and conflict arise.

Watch Out for the Dreaded MFAS

Do you know the person who always has the answer to every question, even the ones that were never asked? Or the person who always feels the need to chime in with their opinion whether it was requested or not? Sure you do. We all know this person. Some of you reading this have actually been that person. I was this person for a long time. It's a terrible affliction that a lot of people I know suffer from. I've coined the term MFAS (male/female answer syndrome) to describe it. It is a powerful disease (I'm not a doctor, but it feels like a disease) and left untreated it can be the death of communication, trust, relationships, and fun. Slowing down in order to understand how, when, and where MFAS tries to sneak its way into conversations is paramount to improving your interpersonal skills and achieving the desired outcome you are looking for in any interaction.

MFAS stems from a stack-up of your brain's *un*helpful default settings. It is hypersensitive to negative inputs, it is easily consumed with the urgent at the expense of the important, and it craves safety over progress. If you forgot these already, go back and reread Chapter 3. Individually, these tendencies can wreak havoc on your life, let them work together and it's lights out on productivity and success.

MFAS usually starts off unintentionally. Maybe you learned a new fact or piece of information and want to share it. Maybe you had an experience (positive or negative) and you want to make sure others do or don't have a similar experience. All fine and good. Just be mindful if when and where and how often you are chiming in.

Your brain *loves* negativity. Well, it doesn't love it per se, but it is hypersensitive to anything it perceives as a negative input. And unfortunately, once you identify something negative, your brain instantly falls down a slippery slope of negativity. You unconsciously feed off of it and if you aren't careful, it's easy to chime in reflexively with something negative.

In the Game of "Negativity One-Upsmanship," No One Is a Winner

The most common area where I typically see negativity occur is when it comes to discussing/comparing travel or vacation stories. What should be a wonderful description of how incredible your trip/vacation/event was turns into story after story of how bad the rooms were or how long the wait was or how expensive the food was or how the rental car smelled like a wet dog. Sound familiar? Pay attention to conversations, they almost *always* go down the path of negativity.

But when it comes to understanding MFAS, there's another interpretation of negativity. This one is the threat of someone else looking or sounding smarter than you. Recall that when a younger animal challenges the alpha male, he gets protective. He defends. He attacks.

The quickest way to combat a threat to your dominance is to lash out verbally, regardless of whether you actually believe the words coming out of your mouth. This is not unlike a knee-jerk reaction, but instead of a physical movement that can be blocked, a verbal MFAS statement ends up in the ears and in the mind of the offender no matter what.

MFAS also shows up in one's inherent desire to be right about something, or about *anything*. When that desire outweighs the ability to listen, or to to be open to or accept another point of view, problems start to arise.

I've seen situations where two people were actually in agreement on a topic, but each person had MFAS to such a degree that they started arguing, just so that each could feel like he was right. MFAS literally blinded them to the fact that they were already both right! The first guy (Guy #1) opened with the classic MFAS line, "Well, you know . . ." and proceeded to argue his point. The other guy in the conversation was equally as annoyed (and stubborn), so you can imagine where it went from there. Guy #2 threw out the classic MFAS rebuttal, "Yeah, but . . ." and proceeded to word-vomit his opinion. The back and forth that ensued finally led to two grown men screaming at each other about their opinion on the matter, unaware of the fact that they were actually in complete agreement with each other. *Ridiculous!*

Over time, uncontrolled MFAS can whittle away at and eventually destroy relationships. What once was a relationship built on sharing and transparency can become one of short bursts of communication that are often few and far between. People will stop sharing information with friends and loved ones, in an effort to curtail their unsolicited inputs and opinions on the topic. People have told me they are reluctant to share vacation stories because they don't want to hear the family member's version of their own vacation. Or perhaps they didn't tell anyone they broke up with their partner, because they didn't want to hear anyone's opinion on the matter.

Think about it, how many times have you *not* shared something in fear of being judged, evaluated, or were just plain not in the mood to hear someone's unsolicited feedback? Now walk a mile in the other's pair of shoes. Are you letting others share?

Are you listening to hear, or are you listening to respond?

Treating and Curing MFAS

The good news is that, like most diseases, MFAS can be treated and eventually cured. This does not happen overnight, but there are things you can be doing that will help reduce or minimize MFAS and help you start leading a normal, healthy life. The following sections offer a few strategies.

Stop Caring about Everything

One of the easiest ways to combat MFAS is to simply care less about everything. Note: I did not say stop caring about things, I said care *less* about everything. When you invest a lot of mental bandwidth into everything, you want a good ROI on your investment. For most people, that means having the opportunity to talk about everything. And having an opinion on everything, *all the time*. That you feel like you need to share. From the other side of the counter, I can tell you that is just straight up annoying.

Specifically, care *much* less about the things you have no control over. Flight is delayed? Unless you are the reason the flight can't take off, you have no control. Let the airline do its job. Stuck in traffic? Unless you are the reason for the accident, remain calm and use common sense to avoid being involved in another accident. Rainy day? I have no words. If you haven't figured out by now that you can't control the weather, put this book down and find another one to read, because I can't help you.

From Robb: I attended a workshop where in the course of the curriculum; we were in a partner exercise in which we were challenged with identifying the worst thing in the world that could potentially happen to us. I was overhearing some of the attendees around us talking about "If I lose my job"; "If my spouse leaves me"; "If I run out of money." And then my partner chimed in with this nugget, "I'm afraid there might be a giant solar flare that wipes out the entire human population!" I'm not typically one to judge, but I might have had a mental white wig on at that moment. It took everything I had not to retort with a "Well, you know . . ." Talk about being overly concerned with something that you have no control over. But then I started thinking about how many people had heard of her concern. How long had she been holding onto this fear? How many conversations had she interrupted with this information? To her, this was a big deal. To me, there was zero value to this statement.

Look for Alternative Perspectives

Perspective is a valuable skill to exercise. No matter the situation, there is *always* another way to look at it. Look for alternative perspectives in conversations, especially when you disagree with the one being offered. You don't know what the other person in the conversation went through in order to gain the perspective they have. Perspective stems from experiences, be they positive, negative, exciting, or boring. Unless you were there to go through the experiences with them you have no idea what they have been through, so be open to the idea that there might just be another way to look at things.

Determine the Value of Your Comment

Like I said, I used to suffer from MFAS when I was younger. When I was in school, I was kind of a nerd. I thought it was important to make sure everyone (including the teacher) had a good understanding of my opinion. But guess what? No one else thought it was important. That led to me chiming in with a lot of very *un*helpful and *non*valuable comments and opinions. At the very least, before you open your mouth, ask yourself (and then answer) the following question: "Is my comment or question adding to or taking away from the point of this conversation?" In other words, are you saying something just for the sake of adding words, or are you bringing value to the conversation?

I had the opportunity to see another professional speaker and he shared a concept that still resonates with me today:

> If it's not important to say, it becomes important *not* to say it.
>
> —Ty Bennett

Man, oh man, have I had to remind myself of that one over and over again! No value to the conversation = No words out of my mouth!

Pay attention to, and please stop using the following terms. They are all dead giveaways that you are relying on MFAS instead of common sense:

- Well you know . . .
- Yeah, but . . .

- A-a-actually . . .
- Well, I heard . . .
- The problem with that is . . .

Pay attention to how you start your sentences. If these MFAS triggers are showing up over and over, you might benefit from going back and reviewing the strategies above. Each of the above lines implies a few things:

- You think you know more than others.
- You value your thoughts and beliefs more than you value others'.
- You might believe in gossip.
- You might be ignorant.
- You might just want to one-up someone.

Try taking an extra second to organize your thoughts before you just barf them out. Determine if you are adding value or detracting from it. Be present in the moment and in the conversation. Then decide to open your mouth. Do this and I'm confident the people around you will not only thank you, but they will start coming to you for advice, input, and mentorship as they finally value what you are sharing.

Get Your Fingers Out of Everything

MFAS can actually manifest itself physically as well. One of the biggest examples is when an individual will do everything they can to help someone even if they help is not required or wanted.

Fundamentally, everyone loves to help. We discussed this in Chapter 8. Here's an example I like to give in lectures: I will pretend to struggle with the title of a movie, giving very vague yet easily solved clues to the film. Things like "There was a boy who lived on a farm," and "the boy had a dog he really loved," and "all the animals got sick," and "in the end, the boy had to put down the dog." Inevitably, someone will scream out "*Old Yeller*" at the top of their lungs about halfway through my list of clues, thereby proving my point that people love to help.

But if it's a situation that people have no control over, oftentimes the *least* helpful thing you can do is to insert yourself into the situation. After all, "too many cooks in the kitchen" always causes more problems.

I've actually seen a stranger push a child's parents away when the child was hurt because they thought they could do it better. And that stranger was so caught up in the moment, she didn't even realize that the adults that the child ran to were her parents. And the parents were both doctors, to boot. Talk about embarrassing!

Before jumping in to "save the day," take a step back and evaluate whether your help will actually be helpful, or if you will get in the way of people trying to accomplish what they need to do. The alternative is jumping into every situation possible, which can lead to people (friends, family, loved ones) purposefully leaving you out of the loop instead of having to deal with you. I'm talking about not being told about vacations, dinner parties, weddings, and events that traditionally you would *love* to be part of. If you find yourself being invited to fewer of these things, double check to make sure you haven't MFAS'd your way out of them!

For some of you reading this book, this chapter is confusing and frustrating. For others, this chapter will literally save your life . . . and your relationships . . . and your career. In either case, mastering your MFAS isn't going to happen overnight. The key is to start small and build from there, which is what the next chapter is all about.

Chapter Review

- Everyone loves to help. Just pay attention to when and where your help is actually helpful.
- Chime in when you can add value, not just opinions, to a conversation.
- If left alone, MFAS can lead to the death of relationships, trust, and participation.

14

Master Your Mind by Getting Micro: Start Small and Improve Incrementally

Big things have small beginnings.

—*T.E. Lawrence in Lawrence of Arabia*

Compound interest is the eighth wonder of the world.

—*Albert Einstein*

Often, achievers believe that the best way to accomplish their aims is to make a huge splash right out of the gate. Sometimes this is true – we talked earlier about how taking care of the beginning and the end of a day or project leads to success. But, much more often than you may think, the *micro* start combined with *micro* accelerations is the best and most brain-friendly way to go about things.

The Hudson Bay Start

What's known as a Hudson Bay Start was introduced to us via British consultant and author Peter Thomson via his audio program *Secrets of The World's Greatest Achievers*. It's had such a major impact on our own business thinking that we wanted to offer an excerpt (reprinted from selfgrowth.com: . . .

> The Hudson Bay Company – which is still going strong today with more than 500 stores across Canada – was first chartered in 1670. Its early history was the supply of provisions for the fur traders undertaking expeditions out of Hudson Bay.
>
> The process they used was called a Hudson Bay Start – they would travel just a few miles upriver (or down), then they stopped and made camp . . . after just a few miles. Now why would they do that?
>
> Well – they stopped quickly because their journey was a high-risk voyage into the unknown . . . and they wanted to make entirely certain that they had brought everything with them that they would need. And if they had left something behind, it was only a short journey back to pick up the forgotten item.
>
> So this stop – while costing the voyagers precious time in a short trading season – was absolutely necessary before starting the major part of the voyage.
>
> So how do we apply the "Hudson Bay Start"?
>
> On the personal front – perhaps stopping for breakfast after an early start on a journey towards a holiday destination! If something has been forgotten we're not too far along to go back.
>
> Or in business:
>
> Say you're about to undertake a project with your team. You know risks are associated with the project . . . so what better than to get the project planned, start to take action, and then stop quickly to assess?

As the leader you might ask yourself these questions:

- After seeing them in action, do I have the right people on board for this project?
- Have they demonstrated the right attitude?
- Do we have the resources needed to achieve what we've set out to accomplish?
- Or did we simply forget something important?

And a question we can use both personally and commercially:

- Is this the right goal?

So often I've seen people not stopping and measuring soon enough on their journey and finding out that the time spent toward achieving a goal has been time that could have been spent differently.

In selling and in business, one of my own expressions is: "Time and distance traveled compounds the effect of error!"

This is the same thinking process as the Hudson Bay Start. Let's stop and measure sooner to make certain we can correct any errors in the course . . . or go back and collect what we need to be able to complete the task.

Too Much, Too Fast

How often have you seen (or been?) someone who got a career off to a blazing fast start, only to fizzle out halfway through the first year and then totally miss the goals? How often have you seen (or been on) a team who played superbly in the first half of a game, only to get chased down in the second half and lose? How often have you seen (or been) someone who got on an exercise kick, worked out too hard or too much, and promptly injured themselves?

Us, too – we've been in all those places, and it's not fun. Getting off to a blazing fast start at anything is great, but then we all know it's ultimately not how you start, it's how you finish that matters. And there can be some pitfalls in pursuing "too much, too fast". If you're not careful, your hot start can be the root cause of a cold finish, or sometimes not being able to finish at all. Our principle of slowing down to speed up fits in with the notion of the Hudson Bay Start, and this chapter demonstrates how that principle can work. Starting fast can be an advantage sometime, but there's definitely such a thing as a "too-fast" start. Here are some of the problems with the "too-fast" start.

Mind Trap #1: The Too-Fast Start Can Wear You Out

Roger's experience running his first marathon is both telling and totally stereotypical. When he turned 40, he wanted to do something big, symbolic, and physical, so he signed up for the Madison Marathon: 26.2 miles. Having never run a distance race at all, this was a major undertaking. He trained seriously for four months, steadily building weekly mileage, until he arrived at the starting line and felt really good. Too good, in fact.

Roger writes:

The thing about a full 26.2-mile marathon is that:

- You cannot fake it—it's hard enough that deficiencies in your training *will* show up and bite you. So I trained.
- If you've trained (which I did), you will feel totally unstoppable at the start of the race.

At the beginning of a good-sized marathon, there's a *lot* of energy flowing. There are thousands of runners chomping at the bit, there are thousands more spectators cheering, "Eye of the Tiger" is blasting on the speakers . . . it's really quite awesome. The air is electric . . . The gun goes off and there's a *surge* of humanity out of the gate.

In your training you'll have done dozens of 8- to 12-mile runs, so that alone allows you to feel really terrific for the first 8–12 miles, and absolutely superhuman for the first 6. Combine that with all the energy that's on the scene *and* the excitement of "Holy cow, I'm finally *doing this!*" and it's very easy to just cut loose too soon.

Which is what I did. Try as I might to pace myself, running felt so amazingly good right then that I just started flying down the course. Hooting and hollering, high-fiving everyone in sight, juking and jiving . . . quite the spectacle, actually.

That initial high lasted for a good four miles. Then some adrenaline and endorphins kicked in and carried me through around mile 8. So a third of the way in, I was way ahead of my "race pace" and feeling fabulous. Even at the almost halfway point (mile 13) I was still on pace to run well under my goal time of four hours. Unfortunately I was about to learn I had unwittingly fallen into the trap of "going out too fast." It started getting ugly fast . . .

Mile 13.1 (exact halfway point of the race): A spectator offers me a beer and it sounds way better than it should.

Mile 15: I experience mild stomach cramps and the rapidly growing feeling of "uh-oh."

Mile 16: Starting to feel woozy, I remark to my running buddy (who's a three-time ironman competitor), "Bro, I'm really not feeling good." He pats me on the back and tells me I can make it.

Mile 17: I begin to lose vision in both eyes. When I tell my buddy "Hey, I can't see," he asks, "Are your eyes open?"

Mile 17.1: After using my finger to check, I say "Yes, eyes are open, but I can't see." He indicates that perhaps we should walk a little. My knees get extremely wobbly.

Mile 17.2: I try to sit down gently to rest, but instead I lose total control of my body. I fully faceplant into the well-manicured lawn of a funeral home. I roll over onto my back and am then unable to move for five minutes.

I had bonked. If you're not familiar with the term, I'd run my muscles out of their primary fuel source (glycogen) which causes a temporary shutdown of, well, almost everything. The main reason it happened to me that early in the race was simply that I'd gotten so caught up in the moment at the *start* of the race that I burned up all my fuel. That mistake leveled me well before the finish line and I paid the price.

In case you're wondering, I was eventually able to get up and finish the race (which was a major victory), but it wasn't pretty. Where the first half of the race took under two hours, the last half was a three-hour trudge. Fast start, extremely slow finish.

Why are we sharing Roger's story of a long race? Not just so Roger can brag (okay, maybe a little), but also because there's an application. Running a marathon requires a huge amount of *physical* energy, and succeeding requires that you pace yourself. Roger's overly fast start used up too much of that energy, too fast. Achieving your goals and breakthroughs is a lot like a marathon in that it requires a huge amount of *mental* energy over an extended period, and you'll need to pace yourself too.

Strong starts are important, but a strong start doesn't always mean a sprint.

Mind Trap #2: The Too-Hot Start Can Freak You Out

February 5, 2017 – Super Bowl Sunday in America – the Atlanta Falcons were not expected to win the Super Bowl over the New England Patriots, and they didn't. But they could have, and probably should have, except their insanely hot start to the game got them so far out of their collective comfort zone that they . . . well, they spazzed.

Coming into the game, the Falcons were the underdog – New England was the betting favorite, and rightfully so. The Patriots, led by all-time great quarterback Tom Brady and all-time great coach Bill Belichick, had been to six prior Super Bowls and won four of them. Well-coached, smart, and almost robotically systematic, they were a dynasty. They were accustomed to winning. Atlanta, on the other hand, was loaded with talent (especially on offense), but was young and inexperienced.

Furthermore, Atlanta was *historically* a team that failed in key moments. Sports journalist Bomani Jones, an Atlanta native, often remarked that he would never let himself believe his home squad would win until the clock ran out completely. Jones would often comment, "Until it says 0:00, you have to bet they'll find a way to break your heart." Over the years, they'd broken the hearts of their fans repeatedly.

But in Super Bowl LI, from the opening kickoff, the Falcons were on fire. Offensively, their running game was dominant, every play they ran worked, and they made the Patriots look silly. Equally effective on defense, the Falcons even pressured Brady into an interception they ran back for a touchdown.

Midway through the third quarter they led commandingly, up 28–3 . . . and then they lost.

There wasn't necessarily a specific moment when this occurred, but you could just see the whole vibe of the team shift. They got tense. You could almost hear their self-talk change from "Yo, we're *killing* these guys," to "Wait a minute . . . we're not supposed to be doing this. I mean, we're the Falcons and they're the *Patriots*." It went south for the Falcons in a hurry. The last 15 minutes of Super Bowl LI saw a turnaround the likes of which had never been seen.

The Falcons' collapse and the Patriots' comeback was historic. Many articles and books have detailed the football specifics, so without detailing every play, one Falcons' mistake after another led to:

- Rapidly growing confidence on the part of the Patriots.
- Increasing tension and deteriorating play for the Falcons.

And you can guess the result if you didn't already know. New England tied the game at the end of regulation and then decisively won in overtime – final score, 34–28 Patriots.

Much has been written about the brilliant coaching of Belichick, the poised leadership of Brady, and how the Patriots won that championship, and it's all true. If you understand the mental side of championships, it's at least as true that the Falcons *lost* a game that was in the palm of their hand, and a lot of it was that they started so fast and got so far ahead that they freaked themselves out and retreated back into their comfort zone.

Examples of where we've seen this with our client firms:

- Salespeople catch a lucky break, close a huge deal that causes them to hit quota halfway through the year . . . then they can't sell their way out of a paper bag for the next six months.
- Top producers start "buying their own press" . . . then they lose their edge and slide from the top of the production chart to the middle.
- Companies get so far ahead of their competition that it appears they'll dominate an entire industry for decades . . . then they stop innovating and get left in the dust by their competition.

There's a reason why Aesop's fable of "The Tortoise and the Hare" is well-known hundreds of years later. Raw talent or luck can get you off to a hot start . . . but it's almost a cliche that the most talented get beaten by those who start slow but are dedicated to always improving. When mastering your mind, don't let a fast start freak you out.

Mind Trap #3: The Too-Hot Start Can Make You Celebrate Too Early

> Hard work always beats talent, unless talent works hard.
>
> —*Kevin Durant, NBA superstar*

The last trap of the too-hot start is that it can cause you to *celebrate too early*. You can get out to such an incredibly fast start and get so far ahead that you completely stop playing your game before the game is over.

We thought about describing a few instances in sports in which a team or an individual got out to an *insurmountable* lead and then lost, but even cursory research reveals so many documented instances of this phenomenon that it became embarrassing. A simple Google or YouTube search of "celebrate too early" and you'll be able to watch hours of footage that will make you cringe. In every single sport you can think of – basketball, volleyball, track, football, tennis, you name it – there are dozens or hundreds of instances on film that show someone who was leading by so much that they could never be caught . . . and then they got caught.

Sometimes it's from getting overly conservative and "playing not to lose" instead of continuing to play full-out (watch the last three minutes of the 2015 NFC Championship Game between the Packers and Seahawks). Sometimes it's from losing focus on the small details that earned you your lead in the first place. Sometimes it's from showboating. However it manifests, celebrating too early is the most embarrassing and demoralizing trap of the too-fast start.

The Antidote to the "Too-Fast" Start: Get *Microscopic*

The journey of 1,000 miles begins with a single small step.

—*Lao Tzu, Chinese philosopher and author of the Tao Te Ching*

Understand, Mastering Your Mind doesn't mean you *shouldn't* start fast and strong. We *love* fast starts! If you can achieve half your annual goals by February 15, we're all in favor. If you can come out of the gate with a new idea so fast it makes your competition's head spin, by all means do it . . . *as long as it's sustainable.* Strong starts are awesome, but Mastering Your Mind is much more about strong finishes. It's not fast starts themselves that mess you up, it's *falling in love* with the fast start and then *falling into the mental traps* of the first start that are problematic.

So, what to do? Get *micro.*

Try starting microscopically small and then make consistent microscopically small improvements.

If you're not familiar with the 100-Day Burpee Challenge, you should be. It's a physical fitness thing. We've done it a few times, sometimes with clients and sometimes just by ourselves. It really works. We're not sure if it's actually just a challenge, or if it's really more of a protocol/program/way of life/torture chamber, but it's a brilliant example of Mastering Your Mind . . . and your body.

The rules are deceptively simple.

1. You designate 100 consecutive days, and commit to doing a number of burpees each day (if you don't know what a burpee is, it's a full body exercise, a combination of a plank, a pushup, and a jump squat all rolled into one motion. Google "burpee" for a demonstration.)
2. Start as small as possible, and improve as slowly as possible. On day 1, you do one burpee. On day 2, you do

two burpees. On day 3, you do three burpees, and so on, all the way up to 100 burpees on day 100.

3. Burpees do *not* need to be done all as one set; you can break them up into segments.
4. You may not work ahead, but you are allowed to catch up. So if you miss a day of burpees, you can do them the following day to stay on track.

That's it. It sounds simple, and it is. Simple does not mean easy, however – this gets hard gradually, and that's where the power is for mastering your mind. The 100-Day Burpee Challenge will make you strong, almost in spite of yourself. Here's how:

1. It's ridiculously easy to start. You begin so slow it feels like a joke. No matter how unfit you are, you definitely can do one burpee. One burpee amounts to roughly fours seconds of exercise. This is genius: The intentional slow start is fantastic for just beginning.
2. It capitalizes on your natural strength-building mechanisms. The idea of progressive overload is the foundation for any strength-training program, and improving by one burpee a day does this.
3. It makes you tougher, but you don't even notice. Burpees are really tough, but one burpee is laughably easy. Ten burpees, however, will get your heart rate up, even if you're pretty fit. Once you get to days 10–20, your burpees start making you sweat, but you've grown into them so you can continue making progress.
4. You build strength along the way and your confidence builds along with it. If you were asked to do, say, 75 burpees on day 1 of your challenge, you might be able to do them but you might puke . . . and it would take a really long time. But by the time day 75 of your challenge rolls around, you have enough practice and enough stamina wired into you from the gradual progress of days 1–74 that you can actually knock out 75 burpees—a proper feat of strength—in relatively short order. Truly

seeing this measurable progress does wonders for your confidence.

5. Halfway through (i.e., by about day 50), you're actually doing something daily that you know most people can't do at all, and then you do it for six weeks straight. After that, you've earned enough "discipline points" with yourself, for a long enough time period, that you've actually rewired higher levels of belief in your own strength into your brain . . .

All this occurred from a *micro* start followed by consistent *micro* improvements. Now you may or may not want to attempt the actual 100-Day Burpee Challenge, but if you want to master your mind, find some area you want to upgrade and get *micro*. Start *micro* small and improve in *micro* increments.

- Want to read more? Start with one page a day and improve by one page a day. Two months in, you will be reading a book like this one every week.
- Want to overcome call reluctance? Start with making one call a day, notice that it didn't kill you, and improve by one per day. Along the way, work to improve your skill incrementally as well. A month in, you will be up to 30 a day, three months in, you're up to 90 a day, and you're probably well on your way to achieving your goals.
- Looking to start a business? Do just one thing per day to move that project forward.

Big things really do have small beginnings, and mastering your mind is no different.

Chapter Review

- Consider the "Hudson Bay Start."
- Fast starts are really fun. However, too fast a start can wear you out, freak you out, or cause you to celebrate too early. Watch out for these mind traps.
- Avoid the mind traps by going micro. Start a new initiative with steps so small it feels ridiculous, but then make small, consistent improvements daily.

15

Mastering Passion and Excellence

If you've never had a chance to watch Ray Cooper perform, do yourself a favor and put this book down and make that happen before you continue reading. A quick YouTube search will net you a *bunch* of results. Take 10–15 minutes and truly appreciate what a showman and performer Mr. Cooper truly is.

For those of you not willing to put the book down, here's a snippet from his Wikipedia page:

> Raymond "Ray" Cooper (born 19 September 1947) is an English virtuoso percussionist. He is a session and road-tour percussionist, and occasional actor, who has worked with several musically diverse bands and artists including George Harrison, Billy Joel, Rick Wakeman, Eric Clapton, Pink Floyd and Elton John. Cooper absorbed the influence of rock drummers from the 1960s and 1970s such as Ginger

> Baker, Carmine Appice, and John Bonham. Incorporation of unusual instruments (for rock drummers of the time) such as cowbells, glockenspiel, and tubular bells, along with several standard kit elements, helped create a highly varied setup. Continually modified to this day, Cooper's percussion set offers an enormous array of percussion instruments for sonic diversity such as the tambourine, congas, crash cymbals, cowbells, roto toms, tubular bells, the gong, snare and timpani. For two decades Cooper honed his technique; In the 1990s, he reinvented his style. He is known for the 7-minute percussion and drum solos he performed during the years 1990–1991 for Eric Clapton and for the 7-minute percussion and drum solos during all the 1994 Face to Face Tours with Billy Joel, and Elton John, and the tours with the Elton John band during the years of 1994–1995.

From Robb: I had the opportunity to see Ray Cooper perform with Elton John, and it was single-handedly the greatest display I have ever seen of an individual perfectly melding passion and excellence into their profession. And then I got to meet him and chat with him after the show and it was one of the most amazing conversations I have ever had. It solidified my opinion that in order for one to perform at the top of their game, passion and excellence need to work hand in hand, not against each other.

When Ray strikes the drum, you know when he is playing the drums. However, Ray also understands that in order for him to most effectively deliver the most impactful percussion elements in the song, he needs to be precise about when he enters the light and when he exits the light, so as not to take the focus from the main stage performer. If you aren't aware enough to be looking for him, you likely will never see Ray on stage. But if you do get the chance to see him, it is a thing of beauty. You've never seen a man smile as big as he does or play as enthusiastically as he does. But as soon as his moment is over, he disappears in the shadows and allows everyone else to play the starring role in the show.

This, to me, was a perfect example of passion and excellence working hand in hand. Ray clearly is passionate about what he is doing when playing his instruments. He *lives* to play music. And at the same time, he has honed his craft over decades in order to provide the right fill at the right time. His commitment to being at the top of his game is on a par with the greatest athletes or entertainers or business leaders that we read about.

Like I said, I had the opportunity to meet him in person and the first thing I did was to complement him on his stage presence and how amazing he was at disappearing when he wasn't playing. We both laughed about that and then I followed up by appreciating the passion that he shows when he is playing. His response was remarkably poignant and spot on.

"Well, if you don't have passion, then nothing else you do really matters!"

It was an interesting dichotomy – the opposite ends of the relationship between passion and excellence. Here was a man who for multiple decades had worked to perfect the technical or excellence portion of his job, but he was only able to be successful at doing that by maintaining a passion for what he was doing in the first place. There is a big giant lesson in that!

Passion *versus* Excellence . . . Really?

From Robb:

Having spent almost a decade in the bicycle industry, I was surrounded by people who relied very heavily on their passion for the industry and the activity in order to execute their job. Excellence fell by the wayside or was ignored completely. Instead of a melding of passion and excellence, it turned into passion *versus* excellence. I was definitely one of these people for many years. However, I came to find out that, like myself, many people who try to use passion as a crutch to overcompensate for a lack of excellence don't last long.

I was of the opinion that loving cycling and loving the industry and loving the bicycle business was enough for me, and if I could communicate that effectively to a customer, if I could transfer my enthusiasm and excitement to them, it would help them become passionate about cycling, as well. And if I dropped the ball or screwed up or didn't execute, it was okay. After all, I was so passionate about what I did that I could make up for any shortfalls in my execution with enthusiasm. Boy, was I wrong.

Then I had a chance to meet some C-suite people who were very focused on excellence. It was all about KPIs and lead activities and ROIs and the other buzzwords that come up in all those fun, business-jargon drinking games. I felt a huge disconnect with all these people and I'm sure the feeling was absolutely mutual.

It's Not "*Or*". . . It's "*And*"!

Operating in the sweet spot between passion and excellence should be the goal of any human being, let alone any professional. Having spoken with literally hundreds of people who are focused on passion and hundreds more who have been focused on excellence, I've found that figuring out how to integrate the right amount of both is the secret sauce to keeping yourself and your brain set up for optimum performance.

I'm seeing this firsthand as I spend time observing the independent bicycle dealer network. There are many shop owners who are very intelligent business people. However, there are also many shop owners who just love to ride and want to spend all of their time around bikes and riding and the people who love to ride. After all, it's the number-one activity that brings them joy.

But then go to the forums online and spend time in the shops, and no amount of passion can make up for the lack of excellence that people experience. It's one of the big reasons for the decline in independent dealers. It's not Amazon, and it's not a shift in consumer purchasing behavior. It's people and owners falling out of the sweet spot of passion and excellence working together to provide a unique valuable and memorable experience.

Passion pursuit industries like cycling or golf or tennis or skiing or photography are easy examples of where passion and excellence need to work hand in hand to be successful. But there's plenty more in virtually every industry that exists.

Chicken or Egg . . . Passion or Excellence?

So it begs the question, does a passion for what you do drive you toward a pursuit of excellence in that career or does a commitment to excellence spur a higher level of passion for the job at hand? It's probably a bit of both, but you can leverage each individually to enhance both.

Take a look at your current job. Are you passionate about what you do? Does it genuinely bring you joy to show up and do what you do, day in and day out? Would you still do that job if you didn't get paid? If so, *great*! If not, why not? Where is the gap? Is it in technical knowledge? Lack of processes? Lack of experience? Did you just settle?

If it's a job you enjoy and are passionate about but seem stuck in (as in "where do I go from here?"), what can you focus on in the "excellence" world to help improve your situation? Would you benefit from taking a sales training class? Or a presentation skills course? Do you need to join the industry association? Get a new license?

Remember the Symposium for our dental clients? What can you do to create the mental breakthrough you need to execute your job at a higher level? Maybe it's not that you lack the desire to achieve excellence, but you just lack the skills. Remember that skills can always be learned.

If you have a role that allows you to display a high level of excellence and aptitude, but you are not excited about it, what can you do to boost that? Sometimes just the repetitive nature of completing tasks can boost confidence and elevate your level of passion and excitement for what you do. If that's not doing it for you, who can you go to to help elevate your passion? Seek out a mentor. Specifically, someone who has experienced the same path that you are on. Learn from them. Ask great questions and, more important, be open to hear the answers.

Make Your Own Cocktail

So how do you master the right mix/balance of passion and excellence to stay on top of your game? Who knows? It's up to you to figure it out, but one experiment certainly won't help you figure it out. And like one of our favorite motivational speaker lines, you won't find the key to that answer as it happens to be secured by a combination lock.

It takes a "cocktail" approach to finding the right mix for you. Here's what that means:

Have you ever stayed at an all-inclusive? You know, the places that typically are in some tropical location with lots of activities, a beach, and a swim-up bar. The resort *always* has a signature cocktail. It's usually sweet and has a bunch of different kinds of booze in it, and maybe it's topped by an umbrella, but it's not overly strong so as to keep the guests "under the threshold" for at least most of the day.

But it's typically not for everyone. Meaning there are some folks that want it sweeter, or stronger, or with light rum instead of dark, or in a bigger glass. But that variation is all based on what the guest wants to experience that day. Some folks are in for a day of drinking and order the drink a bit weaker so they can have fun all day. Some folks want to go hard, pass out for a while, and then ramp back up after a siesta.

Ultimately, there is no right or wrong answer for how to make the drink. It all comes down to the combination that the guest needs to have the experience they are yearning for. The same thing goes with mastering your cocktail of passion and excellence.

It's never one or the other. There has to be both, but each ingredient needs to be used proportionately in order to achieve the goal.

Working with highly technical, specialized people (i.e., accountants, lawyers, dentists, engineers) may require a bit more use of excellence (data, numbers, proof points, rationality). These professionals tend to rely on data and numbers and proof points and rational conversations. The experience you have in these areas will help you communicate more effectively and close the deal with fewer moments of thinking about it.

So take the time to do your research, practice your presentation, and know the numbers before you engage with these folks.

That being said, you will never get them fully on board with just numbers and hard data. The ability to tap into their passion and emotion can help guide them down the path.

If you have ever watched the show *Shark Tank*, you know that the sharks (the investors) *always* hammer on the numbers with the people pitching. It's all about sales and valuations and purchase orders and dollars. But then once they get all that "excellence" information, it's the story behind why the entrepreneur is there in the first place that leads to them making an offer and opening their checkbook. It's the farmer who wanted to make it easier to grow trees on his property, or the single mom who had an idea of how to make her life a little easier. In most cases, crying leads to buying. As in, when the person or people pitching start tearing up about why they believe in their offer, the Sharks start to make the offers.

On the other end of the spectrum, when you find yourself working with artists, athletes, musicians, educators, or nonprofits, your ability to go off-script and flex your passion muscle (not *that* one!) a little more will help you connect better with this folks.

Tapping into their emotions helps them connect better with you. They are looking for the human element in the deal. Helping paint a picture of what their life will be like with your solution is what is needed to motivate them to work with you.

And then eventually the numbers will need to be discussed. The contracts will need to be drafted and the work will have to begin.

From Robb—I just got back from completing my second Triple Bypass bicycle ride. For over 30 years, cyclists have participated in this one-day event in which they pedal 120 miles, climbing over 10,000 vertical feet over three mountain passes, each above 10,500 feet elevation, with the highest just under 12,000 feet. In talking with people about the event, the biggest question that comes up is "You live in Chicago, how the heck do you train for that?"

The short version to that answer is what this chapter is all about. I was able to find the blend of passion and excellence needed to achieve the goal. My cousin joined me on this event and really benefited from this approach.

It all starts out with having the passion and excitement about completing the event. We both wanted to have the feeling of accomplishment after having completed the event. We got jazzed up about the idea of standing at 12,000 feet and then screaming down hill at 40-plus miles per hour. Most of all, we were excited to raise a celebratory beer in the air the end and congratulate each other.

But pictures and stories and smiles weren't going to get us over those hills. We had to create a dedicated plan to train. We had to physically prepare our bodies for eight-plus hours in the saddle. We had to get our bikes fitted to allow our bodies to be in that position that long. We had to adjust our diet in order to be able to fuel ourselves over the course of the event. We had to research the course profile in order to learn when and where the aid stations were so we could make it to each one without running out of energy.

And then come event day, it was a commitment to the blend of both passion and excellence that got us across the finish line. Passion alone wasn't going to keep me on the bike, and being too focused on the numbers wasn't going to allow me to enjoy the experience. Only a perfect mix of both (and it was a fluid relationship between the two all day) allowed us to achieve our goal.

Ultimately, it will come down to the proportions that you use in order to execute your job at a high level. Sometimes you'll have to exhibit excellence in your approach, with just a flash of flair and passion. And other times you will need to inject everyone around you with enthusiasm and passion for what you are doing, but maintain excellence while you do so. But you will need to screw up a bit, too. You will need to try out a few different approaches to see what works for you. Just like trying a new drink for the very first time: you may not like it at first, but over time you will tweak the recipe and try it again and again until you discover the right combination that works for you. And at that point, you will have become a success mixologist master.

Chapter Review

- It's passion and excellence that lead to success, not one or the other.
- Passion is not a substitute for skill.
- Make a passion/excellence cocktail that works for you and your audience.

Conclusion

Next Steps: What to Do from Here?

Every new beginning comes from some other beginning's end.

—*Seneca*

Lather, rinse, repeat.

—*Label on the bottle of shampoo*

So we're approaching the end of this part of our journey together; we trust you've gained some understanding of yourself, and developed or adopted some solid strategies for making your world better.

In book-writing terms, this is supposed to be the "conclusion," but we find that reaching the final pages of a book like *Master Your Mind* is at least as much of a beginning point as an ending. Corny as that may sound, it's the truth. Mastering your mind is much more of a process than an event, so let's use these final pages to recap, review, and then move forward.

Back in the introduction, we'd encouraged you to look for a small number of new understandings or action steps to get going on quickly. Remember how many we said constitutes a "small number"? Right . . . one or two. So take a moment and consider what *your* one or two things might be. There are a ton to choose from, we've served up a *ton*. Likely it's taken you at least several days, maybe even several weeks with us to reach this point. So it would actually be really smart to flip back through these pages right now and see your highlights and notes. In case you don't have the time or ability to do this right now, here's a quick bullet-pointed synopsis, free-association style:

You started out hearing how Roger got left in the dust by a four-foot grandma, then how Robb was feeling left out during BOOM-BAH and HEY! Then you got some tips on how to use this book, including a not-so-small lesson on how the "majority" is usually wrong.

Then you got the actual chapters: Part I gave you some good foundational and scientific understandings.

Chapter 1: Slowing Down, Speeding Up, and Your "Runaway Brain": What Are We Talking About?

- Slowing down means ...
- Getting results faster means ...
- How your brain runs away

Chapter 2: Understanding Your Subconscious

- Conscious Ant, subconscious Elephant
- Your two brains speak different languages (not like Spanish and Italian, more like French and German)
- Clarity is king
- Your brain is like a preschooler . . . *no* doesn't register
- What versus why versus how

Chapter 3: Understanding Your Brain-Wave Patterns

- You don't have broccoli in your teeth, but your brain is vibrating
- Sympathetic resonance and the law of attraction
- The fraternity of Beta Alpha Theta Delta
- Beginning and end of your day are *critical*

Chapter 4: Your Brain's Unhelpful Default Settings

- You're not a bad person, but your survival mechanisms don't work so well any more
- Your brain overemphasizes the negative
- Your brain is easily consumed with the urgent
- Your brain craves safety

Chapter 5: The 2-Millimeter Principle, and Your Recipe For a Breakthrough

- Small changes lead to huge swings
- Golf balls on the tee and the Kentucky Derby
- Get help
- Get invested
- Get away

Then we arrived at Part II, where we started working on methods, techniques, and tactics.

Chapter 6: Master Your Mind by Mastering your Inputs: Program Your Brain for "Automatic Results"

- Revisited the fraternity of Beta Alpha Theta Delta
- Winning the beginning of your day
- Winning the end of your day

Chapter 7: Master Your Mind by Mastering your Self-Talk: Make the "Voices In Your Head" Your Ally

- Still no broccoli in your teeth, but your brain is always talking to you
- That conversation between your brain and you (your self-talk) makes or breaks your life
- That conversation is either consciously helpful or unconsciously *un*helpful
- "The Process" for molding and impacting your self-talk

Chapter 8: Master Your Mind with the Shocking Power of Clarity

- Embrace the power of not caring
- Ignore those energy-suckers
- Figure out what you are too ____ for.

Chapter 9: Master Your Mind by Mastering Your Week: The Two-Hour Solution

- Take a dedicated chunk of time to have a meeting with yourself every week
- Put on your own oxygen mask before helping others
- Get clear on what you want to accomplish during the week
- Be willing to really stink at the process for a few weeks
- Use the five most powerful words in productivity: "Love to, can't right now."

Chapter 10: Master Your Mind with the Fine Art of Saying No

- We're wired for yes
- Too much yes can kill you
- Say no to certain people, especially those who just suck.
- Say no to certain activities

Chapter 11: Master Your Mind by Mastering Your Environment: Declutter

- Physically declutter
- Mentally declutter
- Cut down your reading workload
- Removing the "junk" from around you actually allows new, unexpected opportunities to grow and flourish

Chapter 12: Master Your Mind by Mastering Your Body: Take Care of Yourself

- Know your limits
- Exercise

- Be kind to yourself
- Get a haircut. Or contacts. Or implants. Or a new suit.

Chapter 13: Master Your Mind by Mastering Silence and Presence: Shut Up and Listen

- Resist the temptation to chime in with your opinion on *everything*
- No one cares about your complaining
- Avoid the following terms: "Well, you know …", "A-a-actu-aly …", "Well, what I heard was …"
- Agree before disagreeing

Chapter 14: Master Your Mind by Getting *Micro* . . . Start Small and Improve Incrementally

- Strong starts are fun, but it's not how you start—it's how you finish
- The "too-fast" start can lead to a collapse
- Wear out, freak out, celebrate too soon …
- The antidote: get *micro* (maybe even with the burpees?)

Chapter 15: Master the Blend of Passion and Excellence

- Ray Cooper is a stud
- Execution at a high level requires a blend of passion *and* excellence
- Passion is *not* to be used as a crutch or substitute for half-assing your job.
- Different audiences require different amounts of passion and excellence in order to connect with them.

Yeah, that's a lot to digest. Again, you don't need to do *everything* different, but you do want to do *something* different.

So what about you? What are *your* one or two things? Upgrade your clarity? Try the Two-Hour Solution? Program your mind morning, night, or both? Get some exercise? Declutter?

Hire a coach? There's a lot of potential "right" answers to this question, so take a moment right now and jot down *your* answers. We'll even give you some extra leeway, and let you identify two pieces of understanding *and* two action steps. Seriously, grab a pen, and summarize your goals for yourself.

Thinking: New understandings or clearer reinforcement I've gained from Master Your Mind:

1. ______________________________

   ____

2. ______________________________

   ____

Doing: Here are some action steps I'll take to Master My Mind:

1. ______________________________

   ____

2. ______________________________

   ____

The Optimal Performance Mind: 3.5 Gets

Whatever you've identified as your big learnings, if we could wish you one thing going forward it would be that you more consistently drop into the Optimal Performance Mindset. The Optimal Performance Mindset is a state where no matter what you're doing, you'll do it with the highest degree of elegant success . . . it will feel effortless and you'll "make it look easy."

If you wanted to get technical à la Chapter 3, it's a mindset where you've got a high degree of both beta *and* theta waves, or at least that's what it would feel like. It's where you're energized *and* relaxed all at once.

Our great mentors Janet Attwood and Marci Shimoff have coined the phrase "intention, attention, no tension" as the formula for achieving this state . . . and it works:

- Intention: You develop an intention for what you want to accomplish.
- Attention: You focus your mind and your thoughts on that intention.
- No tension: You unleash your power with a strong sense of trust. You "strike like lightning in all directions."

It's a very Zen, kind of martial arts way of looking at it, which we love. Here's our personal description of how to inhabit the optimal performance mind. We call it the 3.5 Gets . . . you want to get these elements in place, and you want them in this order.

#1 Get Clear

In case this message wasn't crystal clear . . . your clarity is your first step, your foundation, your trump card, your "one thing," whatever term you want to use. We said that upgrading your clarity about what you want and why you want that is the single biggest thing you can do to master your mind – do not miss that.

Getting clear means setting a goal, develop a vision, and have a clear picture in your mind of where you want to end up. That picture gives your subconscious Elephant both the guidance it needs *and* the fuel to get going. The Optimal Performance Mind starts with getting clear.

#2 Get Focused

An optimally performing mind is focused on:

- *Clarity about your desired end result*, which we just described. Your best mechanism for this is literally just a few moments of visualization in the morning, at night, and during your Two-Hour Solution. Go back to Chapter 2 to review why this is so critical, and Chapters 7–9 to hone your technique for consistently focusing your mind this way. Focusing your thoughts on your end result even one time will energize you. A little bit every day for a period of a few weeks builds the calm confidence you want to feel.

- *Filling up the "energy tank," and keeping it full.* Regularly focus your thoughts on things and people that make you feel good, and as much as possible avoid those that drain you or tense you up. Gratitude is your surest ally here.
- *The next right step.* When you've got your mind focused on that end result *and* a full tank of energy, you just need to trust that your subconscious elephant is indeed moving toward that "oasis." Your main job then is to listen to your intuition and just focus on taking the next right step. The connection between your mind, God, and the Universe will guide your steps if you will let them be guided. Just take the next right step. After that, the next one . . . and so on.

Fill your mind with a focus on these three things, and it will perform optimally.

#3 Get Moving, and Stay Loose

Nothing happens without action. If you want to reach your goals you will need to take steps in their direction. If your mind is holding a picture of your goals, and you feel good, it's time to take those steps. Take them strongly, confidently, and consistently. Get to work – it's time.

#3.5 Get Help

We talked about this idea back in the recipe for a breakthrough section, and it bears repeating. Get help along the way. Be open to the ideas, the support, and the accountability that can only come from another human being. In fact, don't just be open . . . actively embrace that help.

Would we like you to get help from us? Of course! We've developed extensive curriculum and coaching programs, plus an entire team to deliver it, specifically to be "the help" for thousands of people just like you.

And if that's not the right form of help for you right now, no worries. We trust that your journey through *Master Your Mind* has been at least a good start. Thanks for walking with us for a while. We hope to see you soon.

—Roger Seip and Robb Zbierski

Resource Guide

You may have noticed that we reference a lot of stuff by other people. That's intentional – it's because we "stand on the shoulders of giants" when it comes to Mastering Your Mind. We've compiled a list of the books, audios, podcasts, events, and coaching programs that we've derived learning and inspiration from in our journey. Many of these resources are referenced specifically in these pages, and some may not have been mentioned, but have been hugely supportive to us. Most of them have actually become integral components of our long-term coaching relationships and we buy these to give to our clients.

We'd recommend you invest in *all* of them – perhaps not all at once, but over time . . . get *micro*, right?

Books

- *The Answer*, by John Assaraf
- *The Ant and the Elephant*, by Vince Poscente
- *Change Your Brain, Change Your Life*, by Dr. Daniel Amen
- *The Creative Brain*, by Ned Herrmann
- *Entrepreneurial DNA*, by Joe Abraham
- *Essentialism*, by Greg Mckeown
- *The 4-Hour Workweek*, by Tim Ferriss

- Get *Out of Your Own Way*, by Dr. Robert K. Cooper
- *Good to Great*, by Jim Collins
- *Happy for No Reason*, by Marci Shimoff
- *Maximum Achievement*, by Brian Tracy
- *The Passion Test*, by Chris Attwood and Janet Attwood
- *The Power of Full Engagement*, by Dr. Jim Loehr and Tony Schwartz
- *The 7 Habits of Highly Effective People*, by Stephen Covey
- *The Success Principles*, by Jack Canfield
- *Train Your Brain for Success*, by Roger Seip
- *What to Say When You Talk to Yourself*, by Dr. Shad Helmstetter

Audio

- *The Day That Turns Your Life Around*, by Jim Rohn
- *The Holosync Solution*, from Centerpointe Research Institute
- *The Maverick Mindset*, by Dr. John Eliot
- *Mind/Body Nutrition*, by Marc David
- *The Psychology of Achievement*, by Brian Tracy
- *The Psychology of Selling*, by Brian Tracy *Unlimited* Power, by Tony Robbins

Video

- *The Secret*, from Rhonda Byrne
- *Train Your Brain Weekly*, from Freedom Personal Development
- *What the Bleep Do We Know?*

Events/Seminars/Speakers

- *The Successful Life Course*, with Ed Foreman and Earlene Vining
- *Train Your Brain LIVE*, from Freedom Personal Development
- *Unleash the Power Within*, from Tony Robbins

Coaching/Mentoring Programs

- *The Enlightened Bestseller Mastermind*, from Janet Attwood, Chris Attwood, Marci Shimoff, and Geoff Affleck.
- *The Holosync Solution, from Centerpointe Research Institute.* (We recommended this title as an audio course, too. Holosync is an audio meditation technology that goes wa-a-ay beyond the typical audio that you just listen to in your car or on the treadmill.)
- *Leader's EDGE coaching*, also from Southwestern.
- *Strategic Coach* – Dan Sullivan is a genius.
- *The PACT* (Personal Accountability Coaching and Training) program, from Freedom Personal Development. (Obviously we're a little biased, but our own company has impacted our coaching clients powerfully. If you don't like us listing our own coaching as a resource at this point in our relationship, that's more of a you problem.)
- *Top Producer's EDGE coaching*, from Southwestern Coaching.
- *The 12-Month Sales Excellence Coaching*, from Freedom Personal Development (again, biased and proud of it).

About the Authors

Roger Seip is the founder of Freedom Personal Development, a global coaching and training firm for professionals. He's the author of two bestselling books, *Master Your Mind* and *Train Your Brain for Success*. When he's not speaking on a stage or coaching his high-performance clients, Roger enjoys being a dad of two, a husband of one, and catching humongous fish. If you're interested in engaging the services of Roger or his team, email info@freedompersonaldevelopment.com.

Back in the day, Robb Zbierski needed a job. After a long, successful stint in the bicycle industry, Robb was looking for a new opportunity and literally ran into Roger Seip at their Fourth of July neighborhood softball game. Fast-forward to today, and Robb has shared Freedom Personal Development's message with tens of thousands of people via platform speaking, private events, public workshops, and personal coaching. An avid father, spouse, endurance athlete, fisherman, and bourbon and beer enthusiast, Robb is also a multi-time finisher of the infamous Triple Bypass bike ride and the Chicago Marathon, and is in the midst of a several-decade-run of never getting skunked on his annual fishing trip. If you're interested in engaging the speaking or coaching services of Robb, email info@freedompersonaldevelopment.com.

Index

Page references followed by *fig* indicate an illustrated figure; followed by *t* indicate a table.

B

D

E

K

L

M

N

O

R

S

T